PHP FOR TEENS

MANEESH SETHI

THOMSON

™

COURSE TECHNOLOGY

Professional ■ Technical ■ Reference

ISBN: 1-59863-139-X
Library of Congress Catalog Card Number: 2006920364
Printed in the United States of America
06 07 08 09 10 PH 10 9 8 7 6 5 4 3 2 1

Publisher and General Manager, Thomson Course Technology PTR:
Stacy L. Hiquet

Associate Director of Marketing:
Sarah O'Donnell

Manager of Editorial Services:
Heather Talbot

Marketing Manager:
Heather Hurley

Senior Acquisitions Editor:
Emi Smith

Project Editor:
Tonya Cupp

Technical Reviewers:
Andy Harris, Christopher McCulloh

Teen Reviewer:
Justin Windler

PTR Editorial Services Coordinator:
Elizabeth Furbish

Interior Layout Tech:
Interactive Composition Corp.

Cover Designer:
Mike Tanamachi

CD-ROM Producer:
Brandon Penticuff

Indexer:
Sharon Shock

Proofreader:
Megan Wade

THOMSON
COURSE TECHNOLOGY
Professional ■ Technical ■ Reference

Thomson Course Technology PTR,
a division of Thomson Course Technology
25 Thomson Place
Boston, MA 02210
http://www.courseptr.com

ABOUT THE AUTHOR

Maneesh Sethi is a student at Stanford University in Palo Alto, CA. As a California high-school student, he founded Standard Design, a web-site design company. He authored *Game Programming for Teens* and *Web Design for Teens* and lectures on game programming at various conferences. You can learn more at www.maneeshsethi.com.

CONTENTS

INTRODUCTION

If you are holding this in your hand, you probably have some knowledge about the web—either that or someone asked you to buy this book for them. Whatever the case, you have found a gold mine! From this book you learn the secrets to dynamic web sites with PHP.

What is dynamic content? Making a site change based on given information (hence the word *dynamic*). Perhaps you want to make a site where you can have several members who all store their own favorite links. Well, with PHP, you can make your site offer dynamically *different* links to each user, maybe based on recommendations or previous links. PHP gives you total control.

Who This Book Is For

You probably know better than I do who this book is for, but let me tell you what I think anyway: You are a beginning programmer, with little or no background in PHP. You may or may not have HTML experience. You are willing to take the time to learn PHP by following this book closely and trying to make programs of your own.

Your experience obviously doesn't have to fit this exactly for you to benefit from this book. You may or may not be a teenager; many of my books's readers are over 50 or under 13. The main thing is that you have a willingness to learn.

What is the minimum knowledge you need to succeed here? You should be able operate a computer well. If you can use your PC or Apple without any major difficulties, you will probably do fine in this book. This book is paced for a beginner, and topics work on a PC, Mac, or Linux computer. I have included information on how to install the software for PCs and Macs, but you can find Linux instructions on `www.php.net`.

If you ever have any problems with any of this, feel free to email me at `maneesh@maneeshsethi.com`.

How This Book Is Organized

The first few chapters introduce design and give a brief overview of the PHP language. You get a fast review of HTML and some PHP form design discussion. You learn about variables, constants, expressions, and operators. Then I begin talking about more-advanced PHP items. You learn about controlling program flow through loops and control statements, organizing with functions, and enhancing web scripts with strings and arrays. Starting with the chapter on cookies, you get into some more-advanced topics. You are introduced to sessions and file handling. Finally, you get to the appendices, which lists all the functions throughout the book, as well as external resources and what is on the CD.

All the source in this book is available on the CD. You just need to install your server (which I show you how to do in Chapter 1) before using any of it. Additionally, some of the figures were taken using different themes on a web browser. Don't worry about the different themes—all of the source files should work as shown.

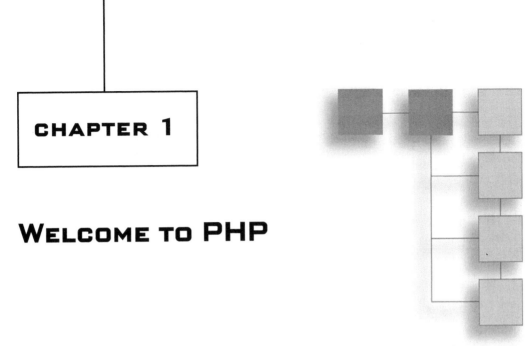

CHAPTER 1

WELCOME TO PHP

Hey, welcome to *PHP For Teens*. I'm really glad you picked up this book, and I want to let you know that you are in for a great ride. PHP, while easy to learn, is also an incredibly powerful and useful language, and this book will teach you everything you need to know to make some seriously dynamic web sites.

So what does PHP actually mean? PHP itself stands for *PHP: Hypertext processor*—seriously. Seems kind of crazy, because the name itself is part of the acronym, like it keeps going on and on forever! PHP is also a current programming language that is often used on modern web sites and development applications. PHP is extendible, strong, and works with many external utilities. PHP is also pretty simple to learn. It is called a *high-level language,* which means that it is between human language (English) and machine code (0s and 1s). Because of this, you can easily understand it and write it almost like normal writing, but it is also strong enough to do some seriously complex things.

So what can you actually do with PHP? You can make the Internet an interactive experience by creating forms that people can fill out and submit and then deal with the data however you like. For example, a visitor can email comments to a webmaster, or post comments on site, or join a forum. PHP really makes the Internet more usable.

To use this book, you only need a rudimentary knowledge of how to design a web site. You need no programming background, but if you have done any programming before, you will understand the language much more quickly. In fact, even if you have never developed a web site of any kind before, you will pick up everything you need to know as we go along.

In this chapter, we are going to go ahead and install PHP. Installing PHP takes two steps. First, you need to install a web server and second, you need to install PHP as a part of the web server. Fortunately, both of these parts are free and on the CD included in the back of this book. The specific installation steps are different depending on whether you are installing on a Mac or a PC. Because most readers will be using a PC, I will explain in depth how to install it on Windows machines. Then I'll give a few hints on how to install it for Macs.

Installing PHP on Windows

Installing PHP by itself will allow you to execute PHP files. At this point you can view them in a command-line prompt. This is rather annoying and ugly, so we are going to take an extra step to install a web server, which lets us view PHP files in a web browser. We need to install the web server first. Let's go over that before we work with PHP.

Installing the web server is a pretty easy process on Windows, because the web server comes in one package and you just need to open and install the files. The web server we are going to use is called Apache; it is free, common, and secure.

What's a web server?

The web server is an important part of using PHP. A *web server* (also called an *HTTP server*) is a process that runs on your computer and sends out web pages when a browser tries to access it. Whenever you go to a web site (such as www.maneeshsethi.com), a web server is running on the domain and it returns the actual page that your browser sees. In effect, you are turning your machine into a web site by installing a web server.

Installing the Web Server

Follow these steps to install the web server:

1. Find the installation file.
   The CD contains one of the files, but you can also go to www.apache.org to find the most current version of the file. Figure 1.1 shows you what the site looks like. As you can see, it's a pretty big site. Apache does a lot of things for the computer.

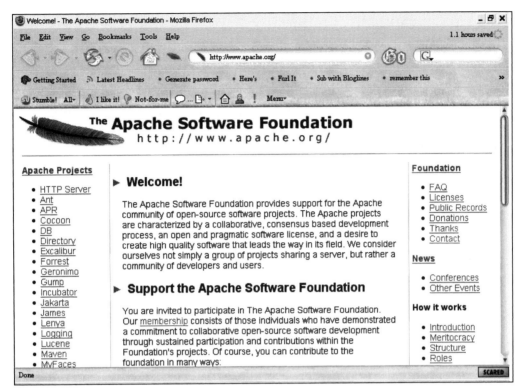

Figure 1.1
The www.apache.org web site.

2. Click the HTTP server link at the top-left column.

   The new page is shown in Figure 1.2. Here is the place you can download the actual server. You want to look for the newest stable version. As of the time of this writing, the newest version is 2.0.54.

3. Click the Download link.

   The new page gives you several options for downloading Apache. They look something like the following:

   - UNIX Source: `httpd-2.0.54.tar.gz` [PGP] [MD5]
   - UNIX Source: `httpd-2.0.54.tar.bz2` [PGP] [MD5]
   - Win32 Source: `httpd-2.0.54-win32-src.zip` [PGP] [MD5]
   - Win32 Binary (MSI Installer): `apache_2.0.54-win32-x86-no_ssl.msi` [PGP] [MD5]
   - Other files

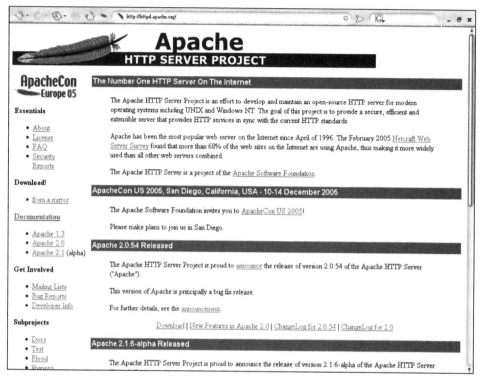

Figure 1.2
The HTTP server web section.

4. Download Win32 Binary (MSI Installer).

   The other options are used if you are not using a Windows computer. You can also install the program from the CD, located in the Programs directory. This will not be the most updated version. Also, you can download the program from www.maneeshsethi.com; just look for the link to *PHP For Teens*.

Note

It's important to note that if you upgrade to a new version of Apache, older modules (such as the PHP module you install later) might not work. I recommend that you use the Apache install file included on the CD with the book, because it is guaranteed to work.

5. Click the Binary option to bring up a download window.

6. Download the file and open it to bring up a window that looks like Figure 1.3.

7. Press Next until you get to the Server Information screen, which looks like Figure 1.4.

   Often this window will be completely filled in for you. If so, you can skip the step. If not, go to Step 8.

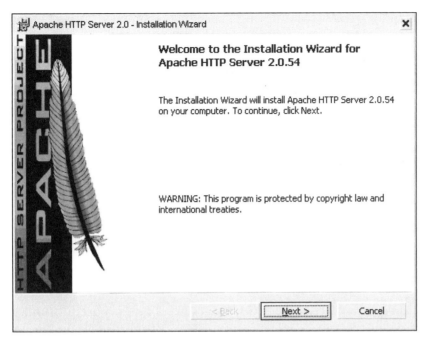

Figure 1.3
Installing the Apache server.

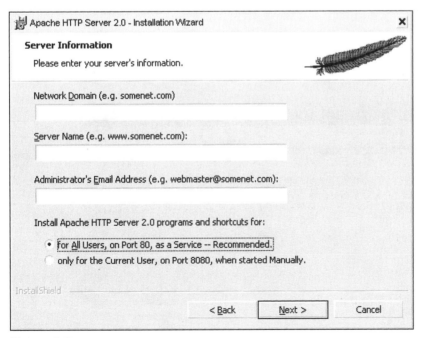

Figure 1.4
The Apache configuration window.

8. Fill in some sample values (for example, `somenet.com` and `www.somenet.com`) and enter an email address you like (doesn't matter which one).
   Note that you can't create a domain just by typing it in. For the domain to work, you must have it already registered and set up to point to your computer.

9. Press Next and choose to run Apache as a service for all users or only for the current user.
   If you install it as a service, Apache will start as soon as the computer boots up. You might get a warning about a firewall conflict with the web server if you have a firewall set up. In this case, I recommend you only use your server as `localhost` and firewall the server completely.

10. Choose Typical Installation, then install it to your computer.

11. Let it finish.
    You have installed your web server! You will notice a new program running in your *system tray* (the area next to your clock on the bottom-right corner of your screen). It should look like a green arrow in a white circle with a feather attached. Double-click it, and a window like Figure 1.5 will pop up.

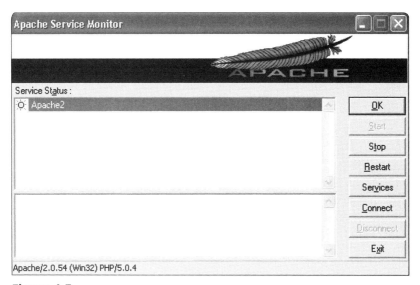

Figure 1.5
The Apache services monitor.

This is the window you use to restart your web server. You need to do this when working with PHP.

Testing Apache

Let's test Apache and see if it works:

1. Open up your web browser.
   Most Windows computers will have Internet Explorer installed, but I recommend you download Mozilla Firefox. You can get this browser from the CD, from www.maneeshsethi.com or, for the most updated version, www.mozilla.com. Firefox is more compatible with web sites than Internet Explorer.

2. Type **localhost** into the address bar.
   Note that I did not include any .com or .net extension. If your web browser looks like Figure 1.6, congratulations! You successfully installed your web

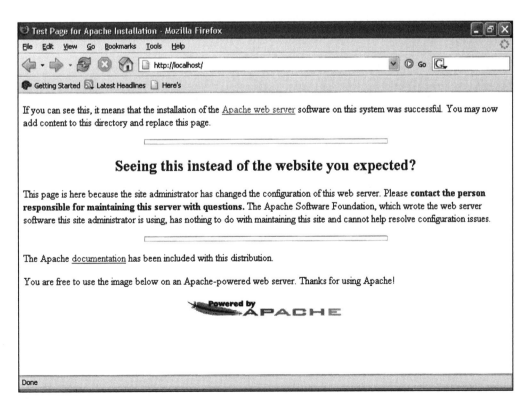

Figure 1.6
The successful installation page.

page. If not, enter **127.0.0.1** instead of localhost. If it still does not work, try installing again.

If your screen does look like this, you are ready to move on to the next step—installing PHP.

Installing PHP

Follow these steps to install PHP:

1. Download the newest version of PHP you can find.
   Check the CD, which has PHP 5.0.4; www.maneeshsethi.com; or (even better) www.php.net.

2. Click the Downloads section.
   You see a page that looks like Figure 1.7. Make sure your version of PHP is at least 5.1.1; older versions are a little more difficult to set up.

3. Choose the Windows PHP zip package to go to the download page.

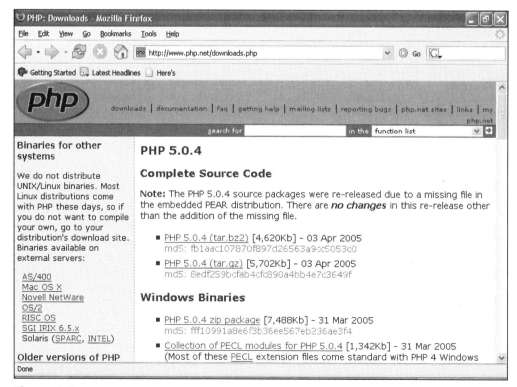

Figure 1.7
The PHP download page.

4. Click the link and download the file.

    The file is zipped. If you have Windows XP, you can open this file by default. If not, you may need to download WinZip.

5. Extract all the files to your computer.

    For the rest of this chapter, I will assume that you extracted the files to C:\php. Navigate to this directory after extraction, and it will look something like the one in Figure 1.8. The next section is a little bit difficult, because you need to edit some text files to make Apache (the web server) work nicely with PHP.

6. Navigate to your Apache installation directory, open the /conf/ directory, and find httpd.conf.

    C:\Program Files\Apache Group\Apache2 is the default location. Go here and open up the conf directory.

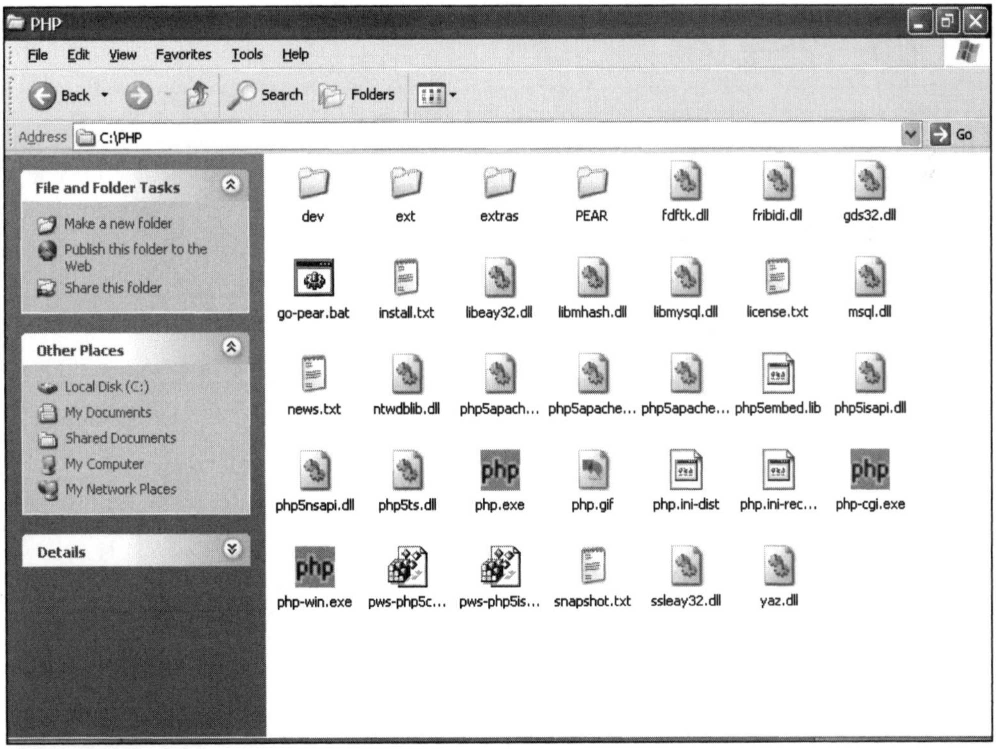

Figure 1.8
The C:\php directory.

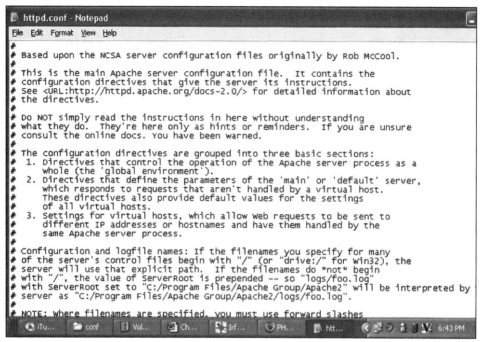

Figure 1.9
The httpd.conf file.

7. Open httpd.conf.

   You need to add a few lines to the document. Figure 1.9 shows what the document looks like.

Caution

Be careful! Two files in the conf directory are similar: httpd.conf and httpd.default.conf. Make sure you pick httpd.conf.

8. Scroll to the bottom of the httpd.conf file and add these lines:

```
LoadModule php5_module "c:/php/php5apache2.dll"
AddType application/x-httpd-php .php

# configure the path to php.ini
PHPIniDir "C:/php"
```

   If you installed PHP to a different directory than C:\php, make sure you substitute the name of the proper directory. All right! The installation should be complete.

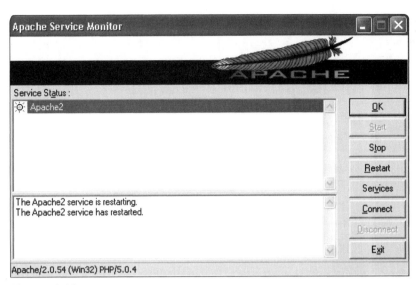

Figure 1.10
A successful restart of Apache.

9. Right-click the Apache icon in the system tray and select Open Apache Monitor; you should see the Apache services window.

10. Click the restart panel on the rightmost bar.
    Hopefully, the web server restarts successfully. If it does not, go through the previous steps, making sure that you did not make any errors. If the restart was successful, your Apache services monitor should look like the one in Figure 1.10.

Note that the window says The Apache2 service has restarted (meaning that your httpd.conf file was properly formatted) and that the information bar at the bottom of the monitor says PHP/5.0.4 (which may differ depending on your version of PHP). If you don't see this, try shutting down Apache and restarting the service.

Testing PHP

We are going to see if PHP is actually fully working on your machine. Remember when you typed in localhost and that web page came up? Well, that file was located on your computer, in the Apache installation directory.

1. Go to the Apache directory, which is at C:\Program Files\Apache Group\ Apache2 by default.

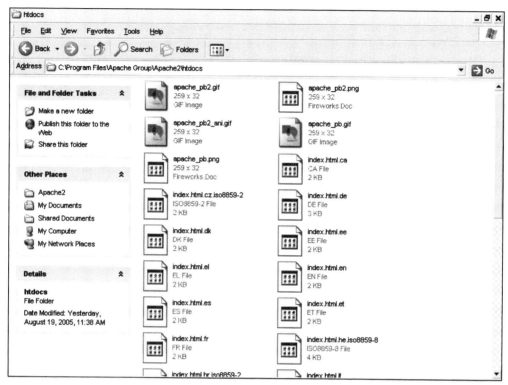

Figure 1.11
The Apache `htdocs` directory.

2. Open `htdocs`, whose contents should look a lot like Figure 1.11.
   In this directory, you see a bunch of HTML files with different extensions. Each of these files is identical to all the others, except they are translated into different languages. Don't worry about them though; you are creating a new file.

3. Open your favorite text editor, such as Notepad or Wordpad—*not* Microsoft Word.

4. Inside the file, type this:

```
<?php
phpinfo();
?>
```

Make sure you type it exactly correct, with the semicolon after the parenthesis. Using Notepad, the file should look like Figure 1.12.

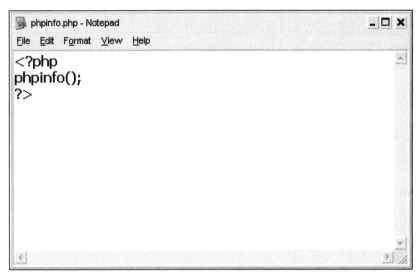

Figure 1.12
The `phpinfo.php` file.

5. Save the file to the `C:\Program Files\Apache Group\Apache2\htdocs` directory with the filename `phpinfo.php`.
Make sure the extension is `.php`, not `.txt`.

6. Open up your web browser, choose File > Open, and find your PHP file in the Apache directory.
This loads the PHP file directly. Depending on your browser, either the page will be blank or the browser will ask you to download a file. Neither of these is good, because you want the PHP code to actually affect the browser. This is where using your web server comes in. Remember how you typed in `localhost` to open up the default page? Well, this time you need to open up a non-default page.

7. Go to your browser and type in **localhost/phpinfo.php**.
One of two pages will open: either one that looks like Figure 1.13 or one that looks like Figure 1.14.

Does your web browser look like Figure 1.14? If it does, then congratulations: You have successfully installed PHP. If not, go through this checklist and double-check all your steps:

- Is the extension of the PHP file `.php`?

- Did you edit the `httpd.conf` file to add these lines?

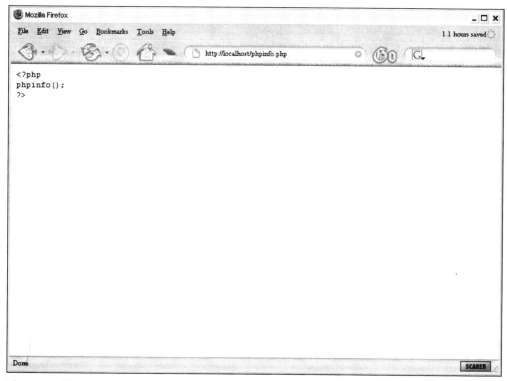

Figure 1.13
The incorrectly loaded `phpinfo.php` file.

```
LoadModule php5_module "c:/php/php5apache2.dll"
AddType application/x-httpd-php .php

# configure the path to php.ini
PHPIniDir "C:/php"
```

- Did you type `localhost/phpinfo.php` in your address bar?

- Does the file exist?

- Is the file in your `htdocs` directory?

- Did you install the Apache directory correctly?

- Does your Apache service monitor give a version of PHP in the status window?

- Can you access non-PHP files through your web server?

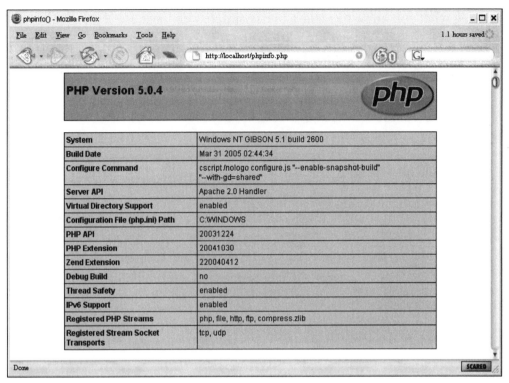

Figure 1.14
The correctly loaded `phpinfo.php` file.

If you cannot get the page to load, the error is most likely in one of these steps. If PHP continues not to work, try reinstalling Apache and starting the process all over again. If all else fails, reinstall to `C:\Apache` instead of `C:\Program Files \ ...\ Apache`. The space in Program Files can sometimes cause an error. Also, check `www.php.net` for ideas on how to fix the installation. In addition, feel free to email me at `maneesh@maneeshsethi.com` with questions.

If the page did load correctly, congrats! You have successfully installed PHP and your Apache web server. You can now fully use PHP.

Let's look at the file you created. Open up the `phpinfo.php` file in your web browser and check it out. This page details all of the configuration options and items that come with your PHP installation. You will see a list of directives along with a bunch of tables that talk about extensions to your PHP environment. For the most part, don't worry about this stuff. These are all default options and you will rarely need to change anything. Just be happy that your installation worked!

Try using what you know to make a pretty simple web page. I will go over how to design this page in Chapter 3, and how the PHP works in later chapters, but for now, load the file phpform.php off the CD. If you want to, you can type in the file directly. The following is the contents of the phpform.php file:

```
<!DOCTYPE html PUBLIC "-//W3C//DTD HTML 4.01 Transitional//EN">
<html>
<head>
  <meta content="text/html; charset=ISO-8859-1"
http-equiv="content-type">
  <title>Sample Form</title>
</head>
<body>
<form name="sampleform" method="post" action=<?php echo $_SERVER['PHP_SELF'];
?> >
  <h1><span style="font-weight: bold;">Sample
Form</span></h1>
<?php
if (isset($_POST['name'])){
echo $_POST['name'] . '. You are from '. $_POST['address'] . '. Your comments
  were ' . $_POST['comments']. ' . <br>';
}
?>
Name: <input name="name">Address: <input name="address"><br>

  <br>
Comments: <textarea cols="40" rows="2" name="comments"></textarea><br>
  <br>
  <input name="submit" type="submit"><input name="reset" type="reset"><br>
</form>
</body>
</html>
```

It's a little long, eh? That is what a basic PHP document looks like, with forms and everything. Open it up! (Make sure you go to localhost first. You need to actually copy the file from the CD to your htdocs directory.) When you open up the file, you will see a blank form that looks like Figure 1.15.

This form looks a lot like anything you would see on the Internet. However, it has a little more functionality thanks to PHP. Try entering some data. My form ended up looking like the one in Figure 1.16.

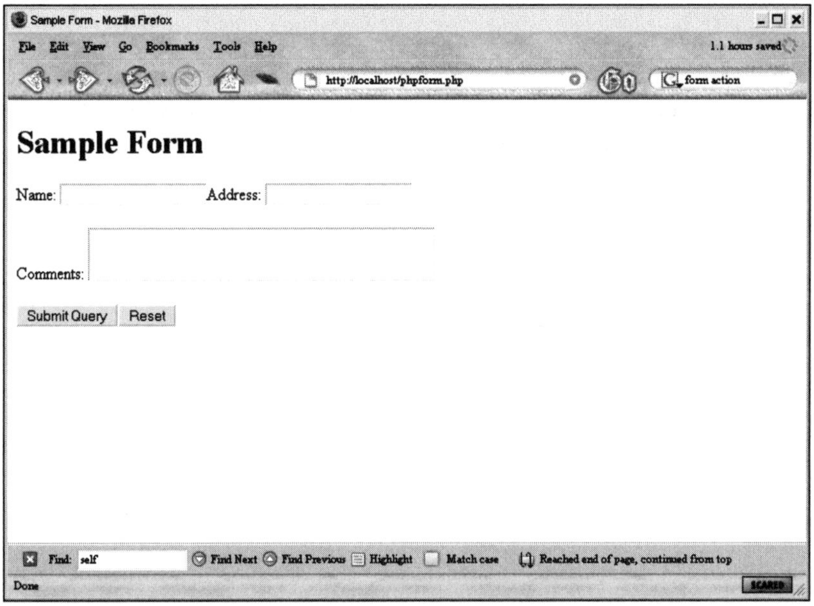

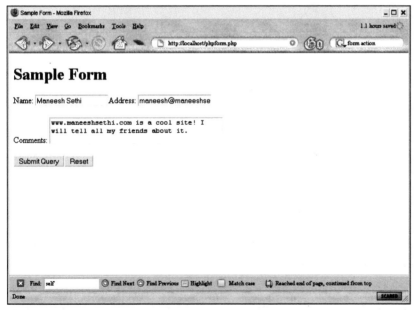

Figure 1.15
A blank PHP form.

Figure 1.16
Entering some data in the PHP form.

As you can see, you can basically type whatever you want. The comments provide some true advice: You need to recommend www.maneeshsethi.com to all of your friends. When you press the Submit button, the magic happens. Check it out. Suddenly the page is transformed into what you see in Figure 1.17.

Figure 1.17
The form after submitting it.

The data actually becomes a part of the real web page! This is one important thing that PHP can do: integrate itself into a page's HTML. Check out the page source by choosing View > Source in the browser. It looks like this:

```
<!DOCTYPE html PUBLIC "-//W3C//DTD HTML 4.01 Transitional//EN">
<html>
<head>
   <meta content="text/html; charset=ISO-8859-1"
http-equiv="content-type">
   <title>Sample Form</title>
</head>
<body>
<form name="sampleform" method="post" action=/phpform.php>
   <h1><span style="font-weight: bold;">Sample
Form</span></h1>
```

```
Maneesh Sethi. You are from maneesh@maneeshsethi.com. Your comments were
   www.maneeshsethi.com is a cool site! I will tell all my friends about it.
   <br>Name: <input name="name">Address: <input name="address"><br>

   <br>
Comments: <textarea cols="40" rows="2" name="comments"></textarea><br>
      <br>
      <input name="submit" type="submit"><input name="reset" type="reset"><br>
</form>
</body>
</html>
```

Do you notice what's changed? The PHP code is hidden, but it looks like you actually hard coded the Name, Address, and Comments fields directly into the source of the document. PHP does not show itself within the document; it shows only the changes it makes.

I spend the rest of the chapter giving tips on installing Apache and PHP on Mac machines, but you can skip them and go directly to Chapter 2, which is a quick primer over basic HTML programming.

Installing PHP on Macs

Installing PHP on Macs takes a lot of checking and writing, because you need to compile the program for your specific hardware. Fortunately, Apache is already installed on Macs, so it saves you a little trouble. In addition, an online PHP module may be faster than the manual way I teach. You can find this module at www.entropy.ch/software/macosx/php. My recommended steps for a manual installation show you how to configure PHP on a Mac OS X (taken mostly from www.php.net). This tutorial uses Apache 1.3 and PHP 4.

1. Go to www.php.net and download the latest distributions of Apache and PHP.
   Make sure you get the Mac binaries or the source.

2. Extract the files into their own directories and run the configure statement through your Mac terminal, as follows:

```
./configure --exec-prefix=/usr --localstatedir=/var --mandir=/usr/share/man

--libexecdir=/System/Library/Apache/Modules --iconsdir=
  /System/Library/ Apache/Icons
```

```
includedir=/System/Library/Frameworks/Apache.framework/Versions/1.3/
  Headers
```
```
- -enable-shared=max - -enable-module=most - -target=apache
```

3. Type the following to set your compiler to do optimization:

```
setenv OPTIM=-02
```

4. Go to the PHP source directory and configure it, substituting your version of Apache with 1.3.12 in this document:

```
./configure - -prefix=/usr - -sysconfdir=/etc - -localstatedir=/var
```

```
- -mandir=/usr/share/man - -with-xml - -with-apache=/src/apache_1.3.12
```

5. Type **make** and **make install**.
   This creates a new directory in your Apache source directory, under `src/modules/phpx`; x is your PHP version.

6. Reconfigure Apache to build in PHP.

```
./configure - -exec-prefix=/usr - -localstatedir=/var - -mandir=/usr/share/man
```
```
- -libexecdir=/System/Library/Apache/Modules iconsdir =
  /System/Library/Apache/Icons
includedir=/System/Library/Frameworks/Apache.framework/Versions/1.3/
  Headers
```
```
- -enable-shared=max - -enable-module=most - -target=apache
```
```
- -activate-module=src/modules/php4/libphp4.a
```

   If you get an error message telling you that `libmodphp4.a` is outdated, go to the `src/modules/php4` directory that was created earlier in the apache folder and run `ranlib libmodphp4.a`. Then go back to the Apache source directory and run the command again.

7. Run `make` and `make install` one last time.

8. Copy and rename the `php.ini-dist` file to your `bin` directory from your PHP directory.
   This is generally done with one of the following commands:

```
cp php-ini.dist /usr/local/bin/php.ini
cp php-ini.dist /usr/bin/php.ini
```

And that should be it! A lot of steps perhaps, but it allows PHP to be installed. Check the PHP web site, however, because you might be able to download preconfigured binaries and skip these steps.

After all of this installation, make sure you check that everything is working right. Follow the testing steps outlined in the "Testing Apache" and "Testing PHP" sections of this chapter: Navigate to `localhost`, make sure Apache is working, load `phpinfo.php`, and make sure PHP is up to date.

Hopefully, everything is working correctly and you are good to go. If it isn't, check the Apache and PHP web sites for hints on how to fix it. In the next chapter, we are going to refresh your HTML knowledge. HTML works hand in hand with PHP, so you need to know a little about it to make decent web sites.

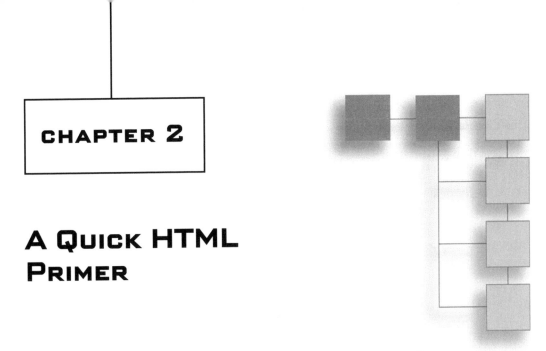

CHAPTER 2

A QUICK HTML PRIMER

If you followed the steps in Chapter 1, you know how to install PHP and how to create a new PHP file. Now you are going to learn how to do a little bit of HTML, which produces static pages, whereas PHP allows dynamic pages. The HTML in a web page generally remains the same unless another process, such as PHP, changes it.

Hypertext Markup Language, or *HTML,* is the backbone code that goes into most web pages that makes text and graphics appear onscreen. This language is basically a set of conventions, followed by all browsers, that allows people to view pages so they look exactly the same in different applications. Because HTML is a markup language, it is a lot easier to write than programming languages such as PHP.

HTML will be used in every web page you make (unless you jump to XML), so it is important that you have a fundamental knowledge of it before moving on. I recommend reading the chapter even if you know HTML; it'll refresh anything you might have forgotten.

We only have one chapter to do this, so I am going to skip some parts of HTML. If we need to use them later in the text, I will explain them then. Instead of dealing with forms in this chapter, you will find pages dedicated to them in Chapter 3. Let's start with the structure of a basic HTML document.

All HTML documents have a common structure. Whenever a web browser sees an HTML file, it knows immediately that the file is a web page and should be displayed as such because of a few factors:

- The .htm or .html extension

- The ASCII format

- The common tags

.htm or .html Extension

By default, most of the pure HTML documents have the extension .htm or .html. However, this is not always the case. Some have .php, .xml, .shtml, .cgi, or others. The web server (in our case, Apache, which you installed in Chapter 1) chooses what actions to take based upon the file extension. Remember when you added the following lines to the httpd.conf file during installation of PHP?

```
LoadModule php5_module "c:/php/php5apache2.dll"
AddType application/x-httpd-php .php

# configure the path to php.ini
PHPIniDir "C:/php"
```

The first line (LoadModule) tells Apache to load the instructions to deal with any .php file, and the second line tells Apache to use PHP to handle any files with the .php extension. Figure 2.1 shows what these lines look like within httpd.conf.

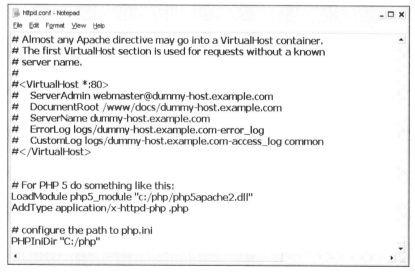

Figure 2.1
The httpd.conf file.

ASCII Format

If you can open up the file in a text editor and you see text, rather than gibberish, then you have an ASCII file. ASCII files are made up only of letters, numbers, and punctuation, rather than the binary bits used for executable files. When you create an HTML file in a pure text editor such as Notepad, the file is always in ASCII format. However, if you use a word processor such as Microsoft Word, the program introduces some weird, non-ASCII information. For this reason, never use any word processor to create HTML files.

Common Tags

Tags are a major part of creating and designing an HTML document. Every file has several *tags* necessary for the page to be viewed in the web browser. Let's look at the structure of a blank document for the purposes of seeing the HTML structure:

What is DOCTYPE?

All browsers interpret code a little bit differently. To help programmers write code that displays consistently in all browsers, and to create a standard way of writing code, the World Wide Web Consortium was created.

To identify your document as conforming to these standards, you use a very scary-looking but benign DOCTYPE declaration. It has only a few variations, and they are readily available to cut and paste into your code—especially since you only have to use it once per document. Let's look at a sample declaration:

```
<!DOCTYPE html PUBLIC "-//W3C//DTD XHTML 1.0 Strict//EN"
"http://www.w3.org/TR/xhtml1/DTD/xhtml1-strict.dtd">
```

This lets the browser know that it is an HTML document: DOCTYPE html. (Yes, even though we are going to make PHP documents, we will declare it HTML. Your server only sends HTML to the browser after it has interpreted and taken out the PHP.)

Now for the important part: This lets the browser know that the code conforms to XHTML 1.0 Strict standards: PUBLIC "-//W3C//DTD XHTML 1.0 Strict//EN". (There are many versions. This version makes your page look the most consistent across all browsers.)

The next part simply tells the browser where to look to find these standards: "http://www.w3.org/TR/xhtml1/DTD/xhtml1-strict.dtd".

If you don't declare a DOCTYPE, you are putting your code at the mercy of whatever conventions a browser decides it should use. Write one! There is no need to write it from memory, either. To see a full list, go to the W3C web site:

```
http://www.w3.org/QA/2002/04/valid-dtd-list.html#DTD
```

```
<html>
<head>
<title> </title>
</head>
<body>
<p> </p>
</body>
</html>
```

Figure 2.2 shows what this page looks like in a browser. As of right now, it's completely blank. However, if you view the source shown in Figure 2.3, you see that the document has some substance. This file is `phpft02-01.html` and it is on the CD.

`<html>` Tag

The first tag in the file is `<html>`, which tells the computer that the following text is HTML code and should be displayed as any HTML document would be.

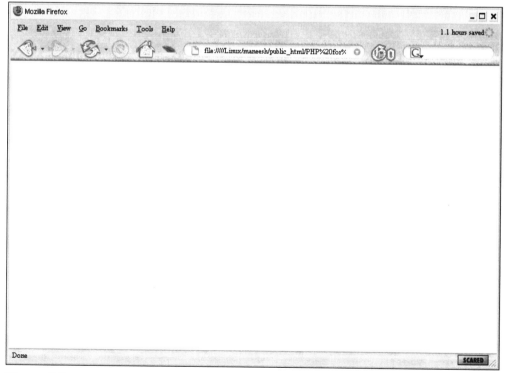

Figure 2.2
The `phpft02-01.html` file in a browser.

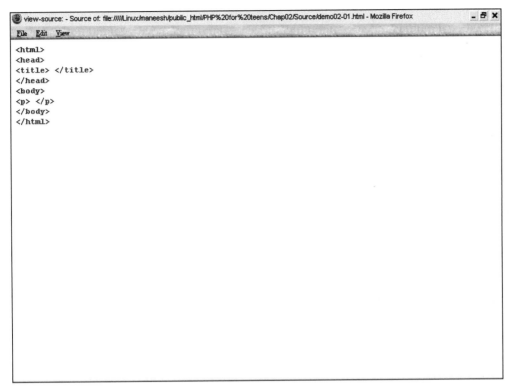

Figure 2.3
Viewing the source.

HTML tags follow a strict set of conventions. Each tag is surrounded by less-than and greater-than brackets: < and >. Some tags have a beginning (opening) and ending (closing); the opening tag is surrounded by brackets and the closing tag is surrounded by brackets and preceded by a forward slash (/).

The tags need to be properly *nested*, which results in the first tag opened being the last tag closed. In other words, when you open one tag, and then you open another tag within that first tag, the second tag you opened needs to be closed before closing the first tag. Let's look at an example:

```
<html>
<head>
</head>
</html>
```

Notice that the first opened tag, <html>, is also the last tag to be closed; remember that the tags that have / before them are the closing tags. In other words, it goes

Sample Form - Mozilla Firefox

Figure 2.4
The title section.

a, b, /b, /a. Be careful with the nesting, because done incorrectly, it can make some weird things happen in your document.

You know what the <html> tag does, so let's move on to the next major tag. After <html>, this is the next tag in the basic structure:

```
<head>
</head>
```

The <head> tag deals with items that aren't actually shown within the document, but are used within it. One of the most common tags is <title></title>. Anything used in this tag is displayed at the top of the screen and in the taskbar. Take a look at Figure 2.4 to see what the title looks like. As you can see, this changes what the bar at the top of the screen looks like. Note that the page title is Sample Form; the web browser added Mozilla Firefox.

Caution

Be careful about putting HTML code in your <head></head> section. The text in the header section is not displayed on the screen. For your actual page contents, the code goes in the <body></body> section.

Next, we come to the <body></body> tag. This is your document's major section, because all of the text and images that appear in your web page are included here. Figure 2.5 shows the body section of the Sample Form web page.

As you can see, the part of the web page that displays all the important information is in the body. If you look back at the structure of the web page that you created earlier, you might notice the final tag: <p></p>. This tag creates a new paragraph for text.

Well, now that we've created a document and set up everything, how do we actually make text appear? Actually, all we have to do is type it in! Take, for example, a very basic web page that simply displays a line of text to the visitor. Well, take the structure that you created earlier, and enter your text inside the

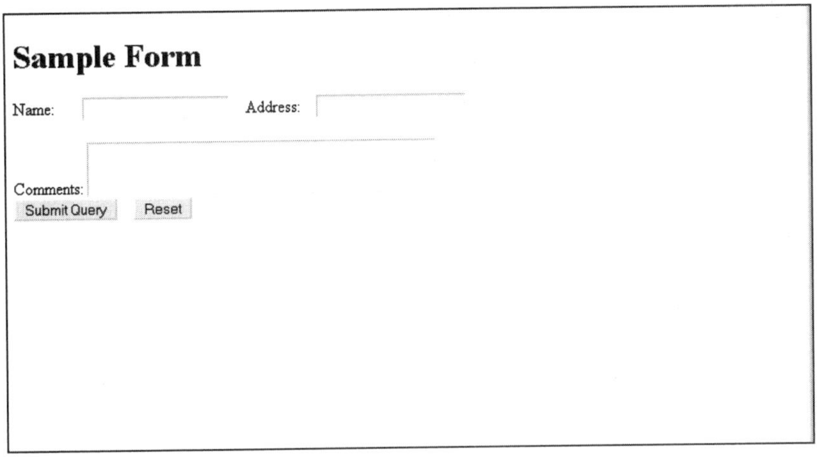

Figure 2.5
The body section.

<p></p> tags. Following is the code that would make a *very* simple web page. How does this look in the actual web browser? Figure 2.6 shows you. This file is on the CD as phpft02-02.html. You can also simply type it into your favorite text editor and save it as an HTML file (a file with an .html extension).

```
<html>
    <head>
        <title> </title>
    </head>
<body>
    <p>
    Hello, World!
    </p>
</body>
</html>
```

Note

There is a difference between this HTML file and the PHP file you created in Chapter 1. Remember how the PHP file needed to be opened through the Apache web server using localhost as your domain name? Well, that is only because the document needed some PHP programming that was executed by the web server. In this case, because the web page is purely static and does not require any HTML, you can open and view the web page by just opening the file in a browser. Make sure that the file has an .html or .htm file extension. Also, if you wish, you are allowed to open the file through your web server using localhost, but this is not required.

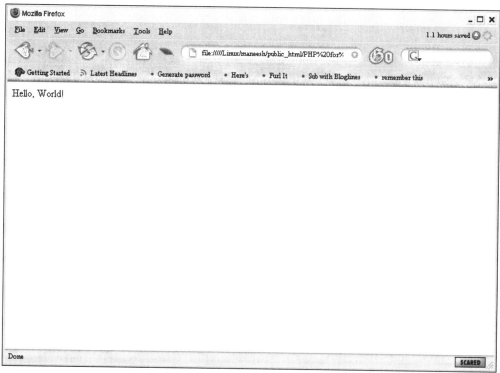

Figure 2.6
The phpft02-02.html web page.

Okay, so you've created a basic web page that shows some text. What if you want to modify that text? For example, say you want to make the text bigger, or make it a heading, or make it bold? Fortunately, HTML has a lot of ways to do text modifications.

⟨head⟩ Tag

Let's start off with headings. A lot of times, when you want to display information on a web page, you want to break it down into easily digestible chunks. You can do this using headings. *Headings*, or *headers*, which come in size levels, make some text larger for emphasis. Look at Figure 2.7, which shows all the different heading levels compared to regular body text. Note that browsers may interpret headings differently and yours could look a little different across different browsers.

You might want to use headers to break up some text. Even this book uses headings: See the "Basic HTML" header at the beginning of this chapter? That tells

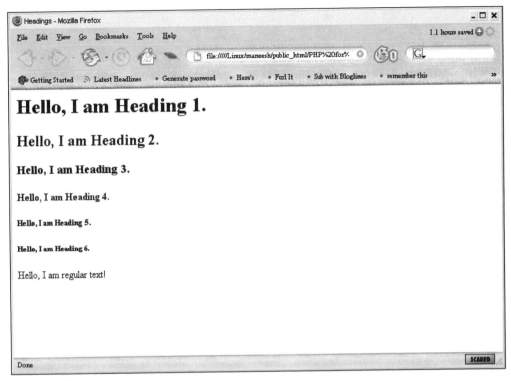

Figure 2.7
Different headers.

you what this part of the chapter is devoted to. Check out Figures 2.8 and 2.9. Figure 2.8 shows what text can look like when headers are not used at all: a big load of text, which makes it actually difficult to read. Figure 2.9 shows what headers can look like when used correctly. In this case, the header successfully breaks up a large section of text, helping direct the visitor's eye to the major section of the page. Not too bad at all, eh? These headers really make viewing text a lot easier. The first figure can be viewed on the CD as phpft02-04.html and the second figure can be viewed as phpft02-05.html.

To make a heading in HTML, you need to use the <hnumber> tag, where number is a number between 1 and 6. <h1> is the largest and <h6> is the smallest. Using these tags around some text will change its size and boldness.

So, if you have a basic web page, how can you change its text into a heading? Simply add the heading tags around the text. For example, if I wanted to make "Welcome to our page!" a medium-sized heading, I might do something like the following:

```
<h3>Welcome to our page!</h3>
```

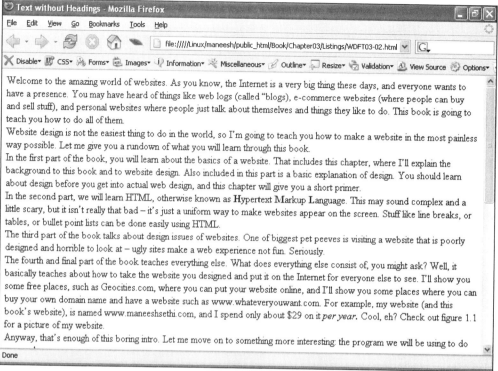

Figure 2.8
The `phpft02-04.html` file with no headings.

Let's put this directly into the basic page we have been building. It now looks like this. (I also filled in the title so it isn't blank.) Figure 2.10 shows what this page looks like.

```
<html>
<head>
<title>Quick Sample Page</title>
</head>
<body>
<h3>Welcome to our page!</h3>
<p>
Hello, World!
</p>
</body>
</html>
```

This page now has a nicely defined heading that welcomes the visitor to the site. It looks pretty cool, huh?

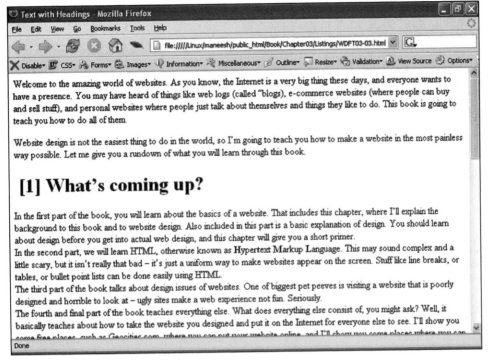

Figure 2.9
The `phpft02-05.html` file with proper headings.

Text-Formatting Tags

Okay, let's do some text editing. At some point you're going to want to change the font or text color, as well as make some words italicized, underlined, or bolded. HTML makes this easy. Let's first go over the easier functions:

- Bolding is done with `<b></b>`.

- Italicizing is done with `<i></i>`.

- Underlining is done with `<u></u>`.

Caution

It is important to note that the `<b></b>`, `<i></i>`, and `<u></u>` tags are considered *deprecated*, or not recommended, by the HTML standard. Because HTML is moving to something called *Cascading Style Sheets (CSS)*, it is recommended you use CSS to do bolding, underlining, and italicizing. The syntax for underlining in CSS is like this: `<span style = "font-style: italic"></span>`. Bolding and underlining are the same, except replace italic with *bold* or *underline*. It's an ugly syntax so I am not using it in this book, but be forewarned that you should design any page with this syntax if you expect the page to be around for several years, because browsers in the future may stop supporting the original tags.

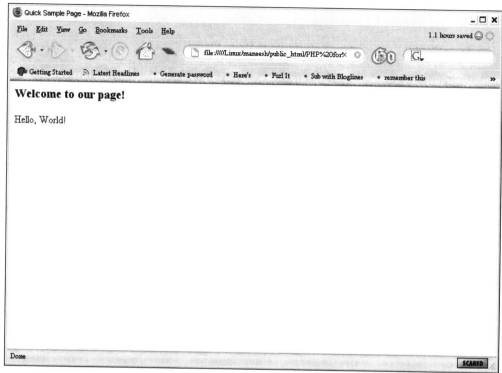

Figure 2.10
The `phpft02-06.html` file.

Let's put some of this into the page. I've added a few lines to the body. The new code is shown here. Trying to visualize what the changes will look like without looking at Figure 2.11 might help you understand when you should use these tags. (I removed the `<head></head>` section to take up a little less space.)

```
<html>
. . .
<body>
<h3>Welcome to our page!</h3>
<p>
Hello, World!
</p>
<p><b>I am some bolded text</b>, <i>I am some italicized text</i>,
<u>and I am some underlined text</u>. <u><i>I am both underlined and
  italicized.</i></u>
</body>
</html>
```

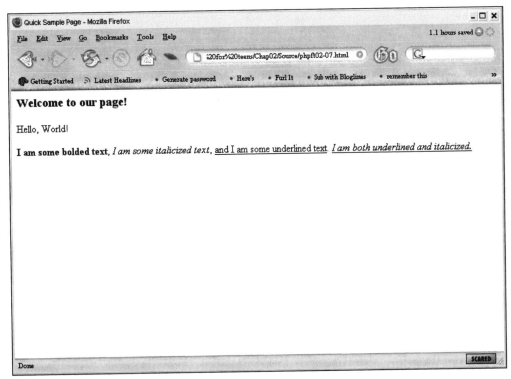

Figure 2.11
The `phpft02-07.html` file.

All right, you've edited a lot of text. Now let's change the font using the `<span style="font-family: " ></span>` tag.

Font refers to many important facets of text. It refers to the face, which is the style. Almost all the text in this book is in Times New Roman. Check out the following however: I am Courier. This is a little different, huh? Besides face, font also refers to the color. You might want the font to be green or red or gray. It's a heck of a lot easier to do that on a web page than in printed material. If I wanted to show you some color fonts in *this* book, you might have to pay well over $40 for it! Take advantage of color when it is free! Lastly, font refers to the size.

Changing all of these things requires the `<span></span>` tag. However, because fonts have so many aspects, you have to use something called a tag attribute. A *tag attribute* helps inform the browser what *part* of the tag you wish to influence; for example, you might want to change the size and color, but not the face. An attribute is added after the name of the tag and is defined with an equals sign: =.

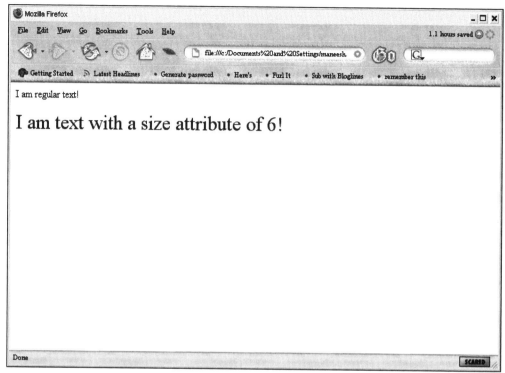

Figure 2.12
Comparing different font sizes.

Say you want to change font size. Well, you need to use the <span></span> tag with the font-size attribute. It would end up looking something like this:

```
<span style="font-size: 18px">I am a line of text that is font size 18!</span>
```

This changes the font to point size 18. Figure 2.12 compares two different font sizes.

The code would look something like the following:

```
<body>
<p>I am regular text!</p>
<p><span style="font-size: 18px;"6>I am text with a size attribute of 18!</span>
</p>
</body>
```

You can change the font color by using <span style="color:*color*;"></span>. The color can be RGB (Red, Green, and Blue) using the proper hexadecimal code or you can use any basic named color, such as white, red, green, blue, black, or orange.

Note

For a list of many common hex codes, go to `http://webmonkey.wired.com/webmonkey/reference/color_codes`.

I need to change the page's background color.

You can do this using the `background-color: color` style attribute within the `<body style="">` tag. If you want the background to be black, you can just use `<body style="background-color: black; color: white">`. Keep in mind that setting the background color to black will cause your black text to essentially disappear. Make sure you change the font color of your text to `"color: white"` or something else easily visible on black.

To change the font face, you need to use the `font-face` style attribute. You can change the font face by putting the face you wish to use within quotes in the `font-face` attribute. For example, writing the following would put text in Courier, assuming that style is available on the user's machine:

```
<span style="font-face:courier">I am in courier!</span>
```

Miscellaneous Useful Tags

You will probably need to go to a new line of text without actually using a new paragraph. The `<br />` tag will do this. The forward slash at the end of the tag lets the web browser know that there is no closing tag.

If you want to insert an image, you can use the `<img>` function. This function, when it uses the `src` attribute, will allow you to insert an image into your page. To add `image.jpg`, which is located in the same directory of the HTML file, you would do something like this:

```
<img src="image.jpg" />
```

Also, if you use the `alt` attribute, you can make the image bring up text whenever the user puts his mouse over the image. Also, the `alt` tag refers to alternate text, which can appear whenever the user turns off images in a browser. Make sure the `alt` text describes the image. You might do something like this:

```
<img src="tree.jpg" alt="A picture of a tree" />
```

This tag does not require a closing tag. Keep in mind the only types of images you can safely display are `.bmp`, `.jpg`, `.gif`, or `.png`.

That last type of HTML you will commonly use are links, which can help you navigate from one page or site to another. This is done with the `<a href="...">`

`</a>` team, where the `href` attribute refers to the referenced item's location. This needs to be preceded with `http://` if you are referencing an external site. This will look something like the following:

```
<a href="http://www.somethingonanexternalsite.com">Click here to view a page on
    an external site</a>
```

Or you may want to link to a different page on your own site:

```
<a href="page2.html">Click here to visit page 2</a>
```

In the next chapter you learn about HTML forms, which are an important part of PHP. After that, you are actually going to start doing some real PHP.

Note

I did not go over every programming construct in this chapter. For example, I skipped tables. Tables are very important in HTML, but not so much so in PHP. Because of this, I only teach tables if you absolutely need to use them later on in some examples in this book.

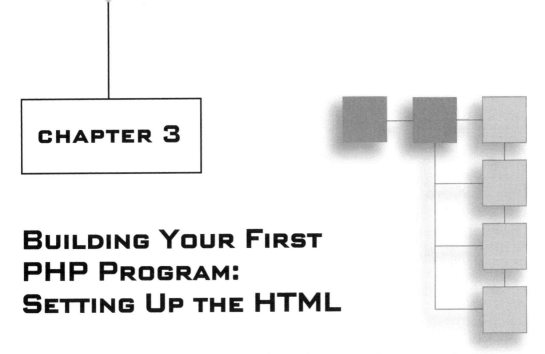

CHAPTER 3

BUILDING YOUR FIRST PHP PROGRAM: SETTING UP THE HTML

PHP is very common on sites that have forms. You've seen web sites that have forms. They're the parts of web pages that look like Figure 3.1. In this chapter I show you the basics of designing a form. You will be using forms a lot in PHP programming, so it's important to know as much as you can about them.

These guys are basic staples of Internet business: an easy way for the user to send information back to the web site. And they aren't limited to just accepting words, either. A lot of times, a site allows you to take a quiz or something that requires you to select from checkboxes and radio buttons, and some sites even let you upload a file. All of these things are done through forms.

Let's take a look at what PHP can do. Just with one line of PHP, I can make the web page turn from Figure 3.1 to Figure 3.2. Pretty cool, huh? Using PHP, I can make it so the web page reflects back what the user typed in earlier.

So how did I do this? First, I designed a basic web page. I'm going to spend the rest of this chapter giving you a quick refresher on how to build basic pages. If you want to learn more about web design, check out my other book, *Web Design For Teens*.

You can develop a web page a couple of ways: through a basic text editor (such as Notepad) or through an HTML editor. We are going to be using a basic text editor to write the HTML for this chapter. Most HTML editors are known as

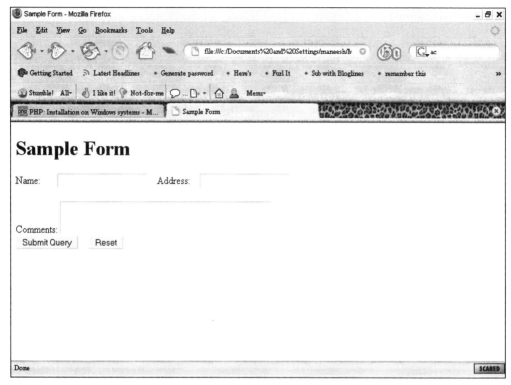

Figure 3.1
A sample web form.

WYSIWYG (pronounced *wizzywig*), which stands for What You See Is What You Get. The editors try to show you the page how it will look on the web site. A basic, non-WYSIWYG text editor, however, shows only the code behind the page—not what it looks like on the screen.

Note

You can get Nvu, which is a free WYSIWYG text editor, from this book's CD or from www. maneeshsethi.com. However, in this book you use a basic text editor.

HTML Template

The first thing you need to do is open up a text editor. In Windows, choose Start > Run, which is shown in Figure 3.3. Notepad opens in a new window that looks like Figure 3.4. On a Mac, find any text editor you have installed (such as TextEdit) and open it.

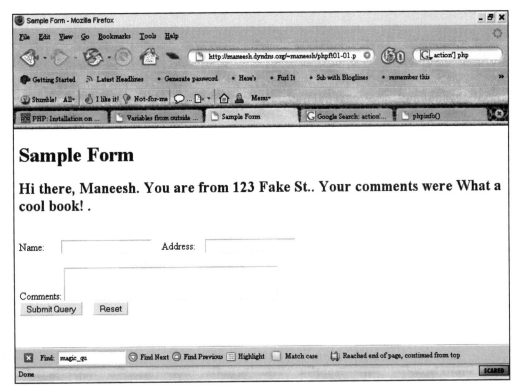

Figure 3.2
A sample web form after adding PHP.

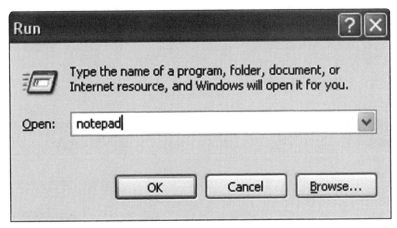

Figure 3.3
Opening up Notepad through the Start menu.

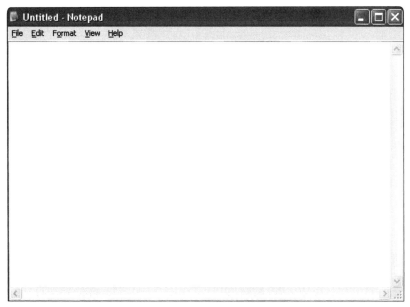

Figure 3.4
Notepad is open.

As you learned in Chapter 2, HTML is made up of tags. The complete template for a page looks like the following. Figure 3.5 shows what it looks like after typing it into Notepad.

```
<html>
<head>
<title>Insert title here</title>
</head>

<body>
Insert body here
</body>
</html>
```

The page title appears at the top of the browser, and the body appears in the actual page space. Figure 3.6 shows the page as typed in the web browser.

HTML Form

Now that you have seen the HTML template, let's build an HTML form. Forms communicate data to PHP. Use the `<form></form>` tag to create a form. (Crazy, huh?) This tag surrounds all of the inputs, such as textboxes and submit buttons.

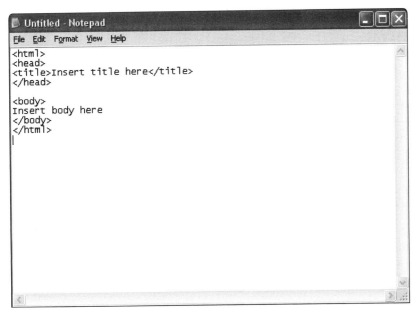

Figure 3.5
Inputting the web page template into Nvu.

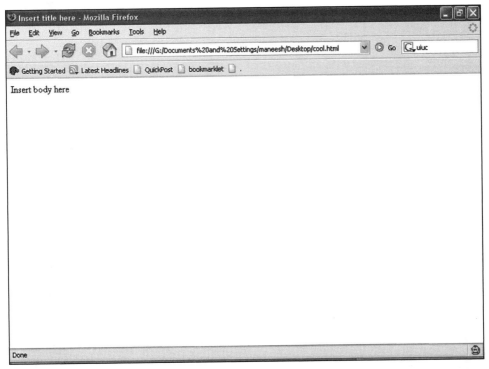

Figure 3.6
Inputting the web-page template.

The actual `<form>` tag itself has several attributes, which are tag describers. Put attributes into an HTML tag like the following:

```
<tagname attribute1="value1" attribute2="value2">
```

The important `<form></form>` attributes follow:

- `method` describes the way the data is transferred. I talk more about these methods in the next chapter.

- `action` explains where the data is being sent. Generally, the data is sent to a separate PHP file, which operates on the data.

Let's define a form, leaving the `action` blank and setting the `method` to `post`.

```
<html>
<head>
<title>A Sample Form</title>
</head>

<body>
<h1>A Sample Form</h1>
<br />
<form action="" method="post">
</form>
</body>
</html>
```

You added some big text that says A Sample Form, which now looks like Figure 3.7. Now it's time to add some form elements. How about two textboxes and a text area?

What are textboxes and text areas?

Textboxes and *text areas* are common HTML form elements. They allow the user to type text directly into the form. However, both of these elements are very similar; for example, take a look at Figure 3.1: The elements after Name and Address are textboxes, and the element after Comments is a text area. What is the difference between these two? Textboxes only allow one line of text, which is not enough space to write something substantial. Generally, it is used for writing small bits of information such as names, passwords, or addresses. On the other hand, text areas can be scaled to any size, even as big as the browser itself! They are great for comments or stories.

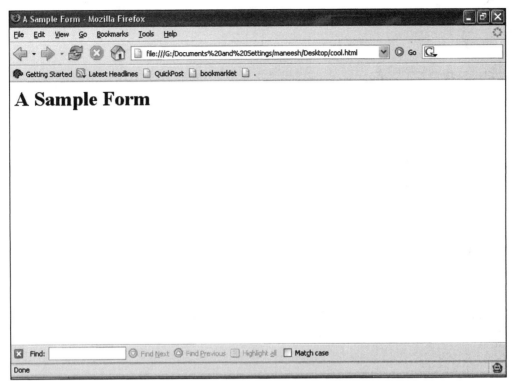

Figure 3.7
Creating an empty form.

Form Elements

Let's make the textboxes first. Type into Notepad an explanation of what the textboxes actually do. This description won't affect the code, but your site visitor uses the explanation to understand what to put in the box. For example, I typed Name: into the Notepad document you see in Figure 3.8.

Now you do the same: To create a textbox, use the <input /> tag with a few attributes in order to make it properly work with the page. The first attribute is type. Type tells the browser what kind of form element it's dealing with. Because you are using a textbox, the type is text. The second attribute you need is a name, which is the variable that stores the textbox contents when you use PHP. Let's create the textbox now. Look at Figure 3.8 to see what it looks like to the user. (Remember that if a tag has a /> ending, it has no ending tag.)

This window shows all the options you need to deal with for any form field. In our case we want to make a textbox, so let's do that via HTML. Add a name to

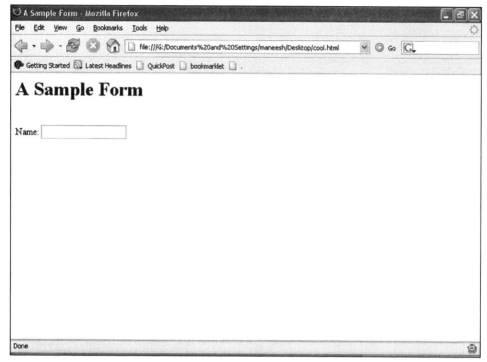

Figure 3.8
Creating a textbox.

this field; I chose fullname. If you want to give it an initial value, add the value
attribute and set it equal to the initial value.

```
<form action="" method="post">
Name: <input type="text" name="fullname" />
</form>
```

Why give form fields a name value?

The option to give a field name to the textbox is incredibly important: Never, ever forget to set it.
Whenever PHP tries to run any commands upon the form fields, it needs to have a way to
reference them. In this case, it uses the field's name. When you need to talk to a friend, and he is
in a crowd of other people, typically, you will call out his name; that is exactly what the code is
doing. Giving the form field a name allows the PHP program to call the form field and use its data.
I will go over this more further on in the book.

Now add the second field. Do exactly the same: Write the text on the screen
(Address:), then create a textbox with the name value set to address. So far, so
good? The result should look a lot like Figure 3.9.

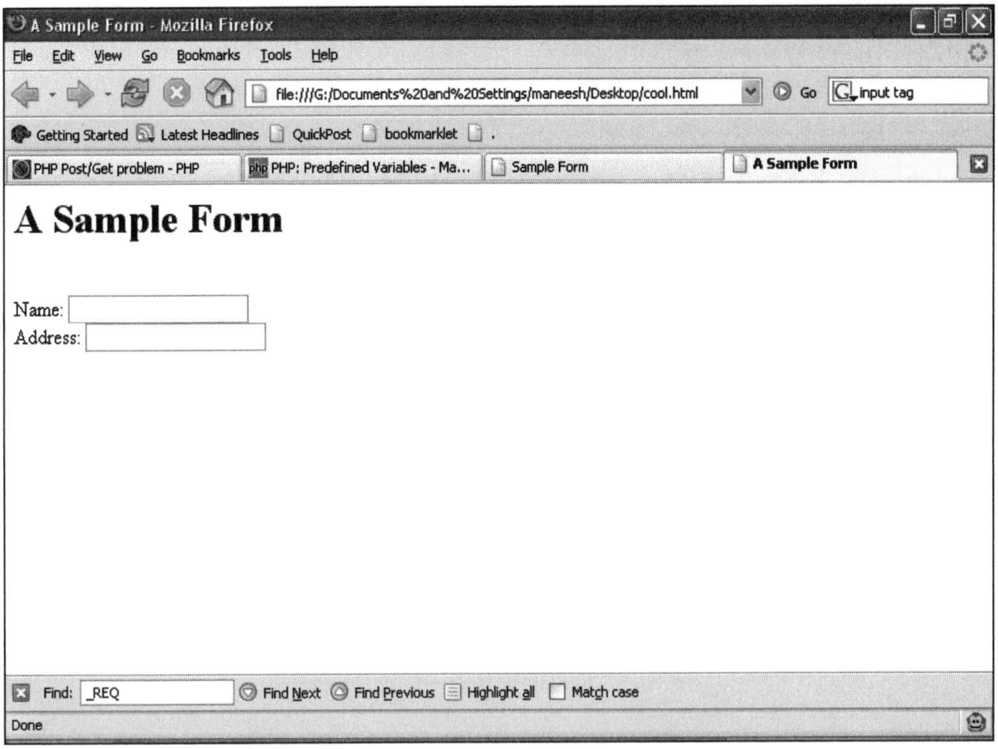

Figure 3.9
Adding the second textbox.

We have just created the beginning of a web page that allows the reader to add some data. So far, she can enter her name and address, but we still need to create a text area so she can put in some comments about the site. Let's do that now with a text area. Text areas are not much more difficult than textboxes. However, they do have a few more options: You can specify their width and height. Before creating the area, use text to tell the user what the area is for, just like with the Name and Address textboxes. To do this, just type **Comments:** on the next line (by using a <br />).

To create a text area, use the <textarea></textarea> tag. Anything you type between the opening and closing tags is the default value. Pretty simple, eh? Let's add the options. Let's give this text area 2 rows and 40 columns. (Each column is one character.) Use the attributes cols for columns and rows for rows. Make sure you name the text area, such as "comments". The code will create what you see in Figure 3.10.

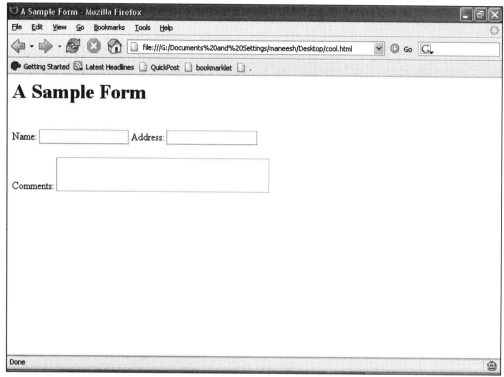

Figure 3.10
Adding a text area to the page.

Note

Even though we made the text area 2 × 40, the user can still type more. When more than the allowed number of characters is typed, the area displays a scrolling bar on its side, just like when your web browser lets you scroll down a page.

```
<form action="" method="post">
Name: <input type="text" name="fullname" />
Address: <input type="text" name="address" /><br /> <br />
Comments: <textarea name="comments" cols="40" rows="2"></textarea>

</form>
```

Submit Button

So far, the user can enter plenty of information. However, you can't do anything with it! The server uses the HTML form to pass data to another program, such as one written in PHP, that will handle and deal with the information. It might email

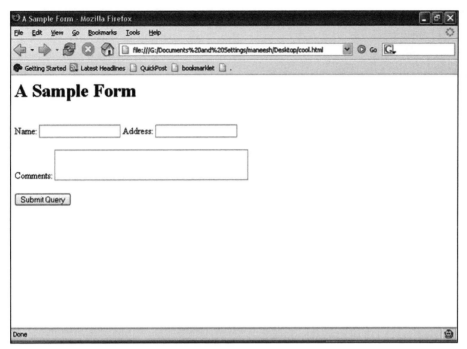

Figure 3.11
Adding a submit button.

the comments to the site's webmaster or it might display them on the site. Either way, you still need to create a way to actually submit that data! This is done with a submit button. When the user finishes entering information, she can press the submit button so the form sends the data to the PHP program to be processed.

Creating a submit button is very easy. In HTML, just use the `<input />` field with the `type` set to `submit`. In most cases, it isn't necessary to enter a name for the submit button because you rarely need to process it, but just to be safe, give it a name such as `submitbutton`. The `value` attribute allows you to change the text on the submit button's face, so it won't say Submit Query. The code for the submit button follows. The page now looks like Figure 3.11.

```
<input type="submit" name="submitbutton" />
```

Note

If you want to, feel free to change the submit button's value. You can make the button say whatever you want by default, such as Send Information or Leave a Comment. Figure 3.12 shows what it might look like.

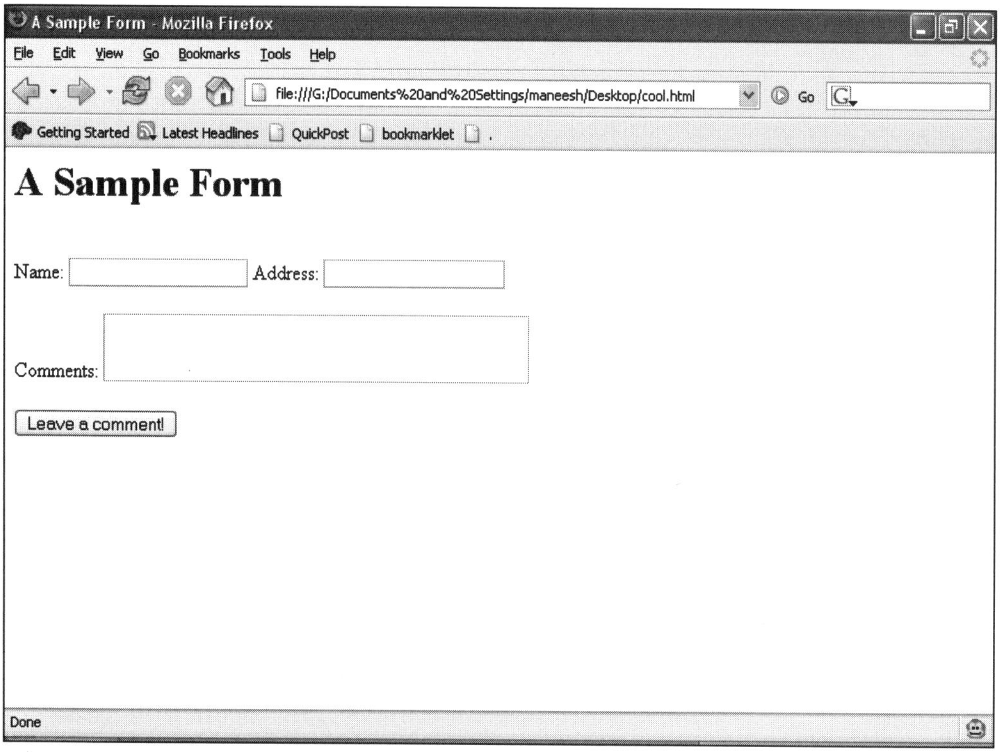

Figure 3.12
A different value.

Add one last, optional, thing to this form: a reset button. It allows the user to clear everything he has typed or selected. Creating a reset button is just as easy as creating a submit button. Use <input /> with the type set to reset. Give it a name, such as resetbutton, and click OK. You have created a form that looks like Figure 3.13.

```
<input type="reset" name="resetbutton" />
```

Adding PHP

We have created a full form. Only one problem—if you open this web browser and press Submit Query, nothing happens! This is where PHP comes in. Before adding PHP, take a look at the source code for the web page we just created:

```
<html>
<head>
```

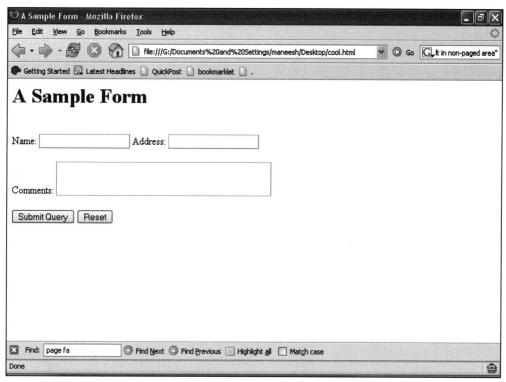

Figure 3.13
The final form with a reset button.

```
<title>A Sample Form</title>
</head>

<body>
<h1>A Sample Form</h1>
<br />
<form action="" method="post">
Name: <input type="text" name="fullname" />
Address: <input type="text" name="address" /><br /><br />
Comments: <textarea name="comments" cols="40" rows="2"></textarea><br /><br />
<input type="submit" name="submitbutton" />
<input type="reset" name="resetbutton" />

</form>
</body>
</html>
```

How does the form know to which page to send the data? It is defined in the action attribute of the <form> HTML tag. Look at our <form> tag as it stands now:

```
<form name="sampleform" method="post">
...
</form>
```

We need to use an action attribute inside the <form> tag to tell the web page *where* to send the data. Assigning the action attribute to be blank makes the page send its data to itself, so the page itself can operate on it. However, this is not useful unless the page is a PHP document. You do this in the next chapter.

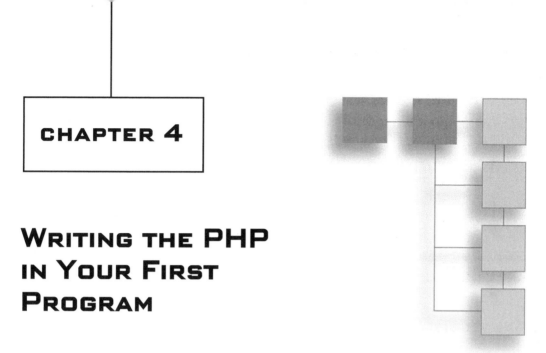

CHAPTER 4

WRITING THE PHP IN YOUR FIRST PROGRAM

This chapter will help you complete your first PHP program and learn some of the basic ideas in PHP, such as variables. Before we start, take a look back at the HTML page we created earlier. The HTML looked like the following:

Note

From now on, we are using a valid DOCTYPE and valid header throughout our web pages. This will get you into making all of your web pages follow the standard. Note that the pages work without a DOCTYPE, but it is very much recommended you use them.

```
<!DOCTYPE html PUBLIC "-//W3C//DTD XHTML 1.0 Strict//EN"
    "http://www.w3.org/TR/xhtml1/DTD/xhtml1-strict.dtd">
<html xmlns="http://www.w3.org/1999/xhtml" xml:lang="en" lang="en">
<head>
<title>A Sample Form</title>
</head>

<body>
<h1>A Sample Form</h1>

<form action="" method="post">
<p>Name: <input type="text" name="fullname" />
Address: <input type="text" name="address" /></p>
<p>Comments: <textarea name="comments" cols="40" rows="2"></textarea></p>
<p><input type="submit" name="submitbutton" />
```

```
<input type="reset" name="resetbutton" /></p>
</form>

</body>
</html>
```

If you want to make the page pass the data directly back to itself, you can generally make it follow this template:

```
<form name="sampleform" method="post">
. . .
</form>
```

We just remove the `action` attribute, and the data from this web page is passed to itself! What does this mean? All the data typed into the form are stored in specific variables. These variables can be passed to any PHP page. Some pages might just display what the user typed, other pages might add two numbers, and so on. The most important thing to remember is that any PHP page must have the extension .php, *not* .html. Rename the page from Chapter 3 firstphpprogram.php.

If you want your form to send its data to a program called something.php, modify the action attribute so it looks like this:

```
<form name = "sampleForm"
    method = "post"
    action = "something.php">
```

Unfortunately, the page doesn't do anything with the data yet because we haven't put in any code that handles it! No PHP in this case is kind of like throwing a football over a wall and hoping someone is there to get it. Without PHP, there is no one to retrieve or use the ball because we haven't created him. With PHP, we can design someone to be on the other side of the wall and tell him what to do with the ball.

How do you code PHP? Well, because this is your first experience, and because I go over all of this in depth later in this chapter, I give just a very quick layout here. When you insert `<?php ?>` tags around code, the web server immediately recognizes that it is PHP info and starts running the PHP program. After the code has run, the web server puts together the PHP and the HTML into one document that becomes the final web site that the user sees. So let's add these brackets.

Add these PHP tags in directly after the <h1> section that says Sample Form. Now our page looks like this:

```
<body>
<h1>A Sample Form</h1>
<?php
?>
<br />
<form action="" method="post">
Name: <input type="text" name="fullname" />
Address: <input type="text" name="address" /><br /><br />
Comments: <textarea name="comments" cols="40" rows="2"></textarea><br /><br />
<input type="submit" name="submitbutton" />
<input type="reset" name="resetbutton" />

</form>
</body>
```

Note that <?php?> tags are not symmetrical like normal HTML tags. The web browser thinks of PHP as one gigantic tag! It also is good to note these other PHP tags you might see: <? ?> and <script language = "php"></script>. Loaded in the web browser it looks something like Figure 4.1.

Well, there is a reason why it looks the same: Nothing has really changed! We have added a placeholder for some PHP code, but we haven't entered any code! Let's do some basic stuff. Enter the following lines:

```
echo "$_POST[fullname]. You are from $_POST[address]. Your comments were
  $_POST[comments]. <br> ";
```

When you see the word echo in a PHP program, the following text is displayed on the screen. In this case, we are displaying the information inputted on the form. Do you remember when we set the form's method to post? Well, all the data that the user typed in the form is put into a storage device called $_POST. See all those references to $_POST in the PHP code? The letters in the brackets immediately following $_POST access the contents of the form element that had that name in the HTML form. So, the user's address was put into a textbox with the name set to address. Therefore, the user's address is stored in $_POST[address]. The entire statement is echoed and the variables are displayed in place of the $_POST[]

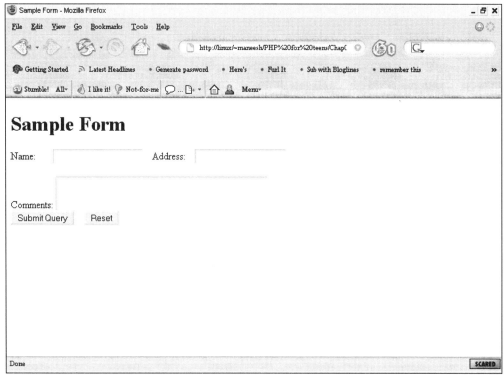

Figure 4.1
The form with `<?php ?>` tags added.

sections. When you put that into the source, your code will look like the following, and you can see the result in Figure 4.2:

```
<body>
<h1>A Sample Form</h1>
<?php
echo "$_POST[fullname]. You are from $_POST[address].  Your comments were
  $_POST[comments]. <br> "

?>
<br />
<form method="post">
Name: <input type="text" name="fullname" />
Address: <input type="text" name="address" /><br /><br />
Comments: <textarea name="comments" cols="40" rows="2"></textarea><br /><br />
<input type="submit" name="submitbutton" />
```

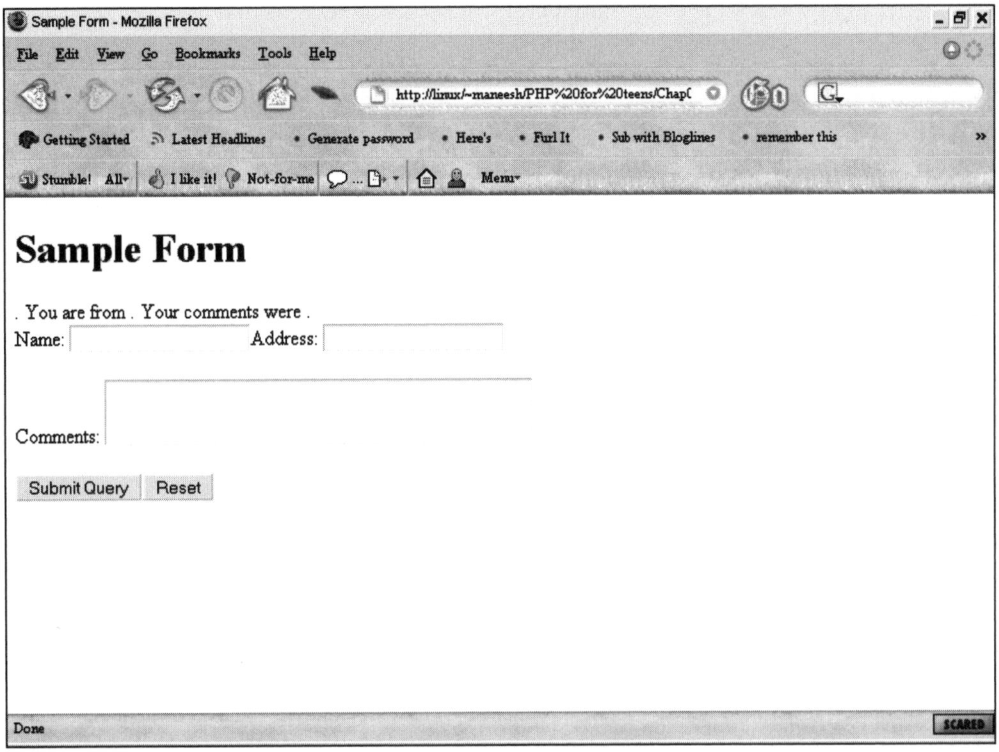

Figure 4.2
The form with some PHP added.

```
<input type="reset" name="resetbutton" />
</form>
</body>
```

Caution

If you run this code on a server with strict warnings turned on, you may get some strange errors about undefined indices. Adding an if(isset()) clause will fix this error. You can see how to do this later on in this same section, just before we start talking about variables.

You see some new words written! The variables haven't been sent yet, so it just says . You are from . Your comments were .. Enter your name, address, and some comments into the form and press the submit button. Suddenly, the page looks like Figure 4.3. Cool, huh? Now it reflects exactly what was said to you! Figure 4.4 shows what the source looks like.

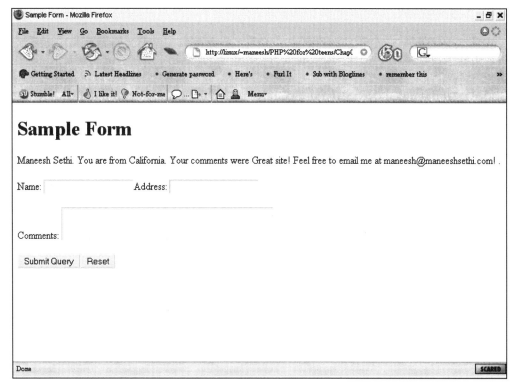

Figure 4.3
The form after being submitted.

Why does the page show '; ?>?

If you are following this program and try running the web page, there is a chance you might get an error in which none of the PHP code works. The reason is that you are not accessing the page correctly through your web server. PHP only works if it is accessed through the Apache web server. In general, you get the error if you double-click a web page to open it. If you find the web page by using localhost in your URL, you will get the correct page. Refer back to Chapter 1 to learn about installation and setting up your web server.

By the way, did you notice how annoying it was that the web form showed a sentence with blanks? Well, check out what we can do easily with PHP. Using a little bit of code, we can make the text disappear when the page is first seen, and reappear when the page is submitted. We need to change the PHP code that we designed earlier to look like this:

```
<?php
if (isset($_POST['name'])){
```

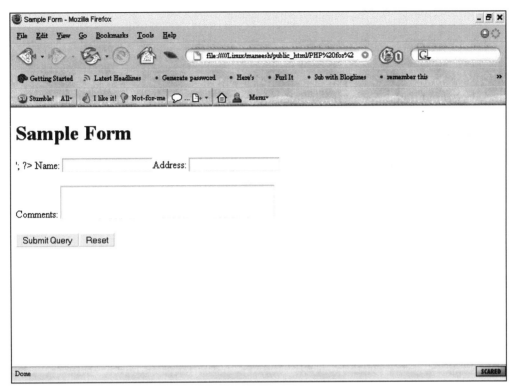

Figure 4.4
The source of the form.

```
echo "$_POST[fullname]. You are from $_POST[address]. Your comments were
    $_POST[comments]. <br> "

}
?>
```

Variables

Variables are the backbone of any programming language—but what is a variable? All variables contain a value that you can change throughout the program. What can a variable hold? Well, anything really. If you want to track who last visited your site to use the form, you can store the visitor's name inside a variable. If you want to create a message board, a variable can save the message that is to be posted.

Table 4.1 PHP Data Types

Type	Description
Boolean	Represents TRUE or FALSE.
Integer	Any number that does not use a decimal point.
Float	Any number with a decimal point.
String	A series of characters, like a sentence or any form of text.
Array	An ordered map that maps values to keys.
Object	A representative piece of a class.
Resource	A special variable that holds a reference to an external resource.
NULL	A variable that has no value.

Types

There are numerous types of variables, and they're listed in Table 4.1. Each type stores a different type of data. For example, PHP draws a distinction between the number 343 and 343.14. PHP handles them different ways, so you can get some weird results when you try to divide a whole number by a fraction, for instance.

Different variables help prevent you from doing something impossible, such as adding a number to a *string,* which is a set of letters. What is 6 + Hello World? I don't know, and if I were programming something, I wouldn't want to find out!

We aren't going to be using all of these types in this book, because some of them are rare and not necessary for basic PHP programming. Let's go over the ones we will use.

- *Integers* are very common and encase a number, positive or negative, without a decimal point. See these examples:
  - 314
  - -2141003
  - 0

- *Boolean* is used for items that have only two states. For example, a checkbox can be either on (TRUE) or off (FALSE). Obviously the following are the only things Boolean types will look like:
  - TRUE
  - FALSE

- *Float* are sometimes called *double.* Doubles and floats are treated as interchangeable by PHP. Float variables (which is short for floating-point variable) is similar to an integer except that it has a decimal point. Some examples of floats follow:

  - `769.124`
  - `-22385.124412`
  - `0.9993858`

- *Strings* are a different type of beast altogether. While floats and integers contain numbers, strings contain text. In the following examples, notice the surrounding quotation marks. They tell PHP that a string is being dealt with.

  - `"Hello, World!"`
  - `"Welcome to my web site."`
  - `"Please donate money to me!"`

You know what a variable is. You even know the different types. All you need to know is how to use them! First, know that you cannot use variables in HTML; you must use them within PHP. As a result, whenever you need a variable, escape from HTML, just like you did in Chapter 1. Remember? Whenever we needed to escape from HTML, we wrote this:

```
<?php
. . .
?>
```

Notice that there is no space between the question mark and the less-than and greater-than (<>) signs. If you don't escape correctly from HTML, none of your PHP will work.

Inserting

So let's add a variable in there now. You can create a variable and use it by choosing a name and adding a dollar sign ($) to the beginning of it. For example, the following is a valid variable-name assignment:

```
$testvariable=25;
```

Using that name, you could escape from HTML and get into PHP like this:

```
<?php
$testvariable=25;
?>
```

Look at that. While we are at it, let's put that entire block of code directly into a web page and see what it makes! The following code is on the CD as phpft04-01.php:

```
<!DOCTYPE html PUBLIC "-//W3C//DTD XHTML 1.0 Strict//EN"
    "http://www.w3.org/TR/xhtml1/DTD/xhtml1-strict.dtd">
<html xmlns="http://www.w3.org/1999/xhtml" xml:lang="en" lang="en">

<head>
<title>PHP Test Page</title>
</head>
<body>
<h3>Welcome to our page!</h3>
<p>
Following is the PHP code. It should reflect whatever PHP you type in!
<p>
---------------

<p>
<?php
$testvariable=25;
?>
<p>
--------

<p>You see anything interesting?
</body>
</html>
```

As you can see, we have a lot of HTML, which creates the page. Then we have a section where the PHP executes, and then the program ends with HTML again.

Let's load this up in a browser. Make sure you load it up through your web server using localhost, just as you always do when you need to execute PHP. What you see will probably look a lot like Figure 4.5.

Uh oh. It looks blank. Well, why don't we take a look at the source to figure out what went wrong. You can see the source by right-clicking the page and choosing View Source. Figure 4.6 shows the source.

Uh oh again. The source seems blank. It's almost like the PHP code just, well, disappeared!

Actually, this is exactly what we want it to do. The web page deals with the PHP code before putting it on the screen. Remember when I said HTML is a static language? Web browsers can only deal with static content, and PHP is certainly a

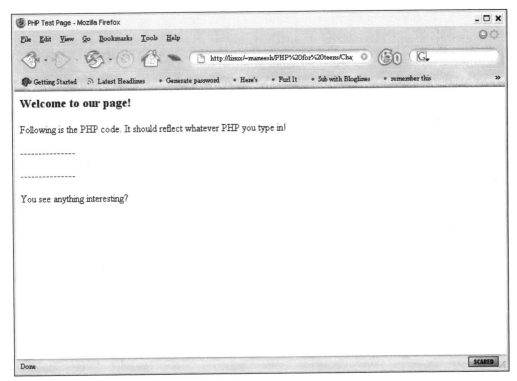

Figure 4.5
The `phpft04-01.php` file.

variable language. Because of this, PHP converts itself into HTML before the document is displayed on the screen. In doing so, it strips away all of the PHP code and translates any important PHP parts into HTML. So, let's take another look at the PHP code from this document:

```php
<?php
$testvariable=25;
?>
```

Looks pretty good, right? But what did we do? We created and assigned a variable. But we didn't do anything with the variable! Variables store any type of data depending on the context, so because this variable is assigned to an integer, the variable has an integer type.

Fortunately, you can do a lot of very interesting things with a simple piece of data like that. How about we make it display the value of the variable on the page? To do this, we need to use something called a language construct. A *language construct* is built into the PHP language and does a specified job. In this case, the language construct we are looking for is echo, which prints out the results of any

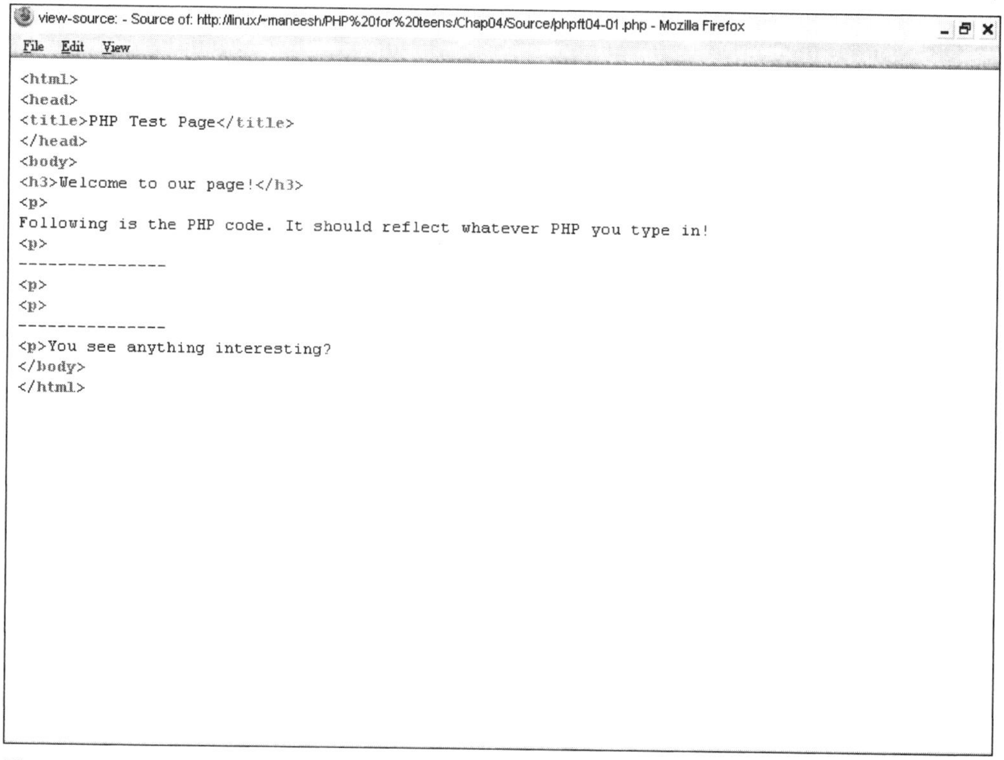


```
<html>
<head>
<title>PHP Test Page</title>
</head>
<body>
<h3>Welcome to our page!</h3>
<p>
Following is the PHP code. It should reflect whatever PHP you type in!
<p>
---------------
<p>
<p>
---------------
<p>You see anything interesting?
</body>
</html>
```

Figure 4.6
The `phpft04-01.php` source.

operation or variable. To use `echo`, you simply type in the construct name within PHP bounding areas, followed by the data you wish to display. You can choose whether to use parentheses. You can decide not to include them and everything will come out fine.

Let's edit the PHP section to use the `echo` construct now. It will look like the following:

```
<?php
$testvariable=25;
echo $testvariable;
?>
```

What's with the semicolon?

If you have been looking closely at the PHP sections of code, you might have noticed that a semicolon appears after each statement. Why? Well, PHP is broken down into several statements, all of which do a different thing. You might write one statement that creates a variable, followed by another statement that deletes it, followed by another statement that reassigns the variable.

PHP needs to know where each statement stops and starts, and it uses semicolons at the end of each statement to judge the ending point. You can use multiple statements per line, as long as you have a semicolon after each major part. For example, the following code snippets arte equivalent to each other:

```
<?php
$example=25;
echo "$example";
$example = 75;
echo "$example";
?>

<?php $example=25; echo "$example"; $example = 75; echo "$example";

?>
```

Variable

The same variable changes to two different values and is echoed both times. PHP does not care about white space, such as spaces or tabs, at all in almost all cases. You can condense the document however much you wish. Notice, though, that the first version of the code is a heck of a lot easier to read than the second one. Try to make your web pages simple and understandable, so in this situation, it is probably a good idea to use the first version of the code.

Pretty cool, huh! Let's see what the results are. Figure 4.7 shows what the new page looks like. Hey, how about that! It works! The 25 we wanted to show up appeared! What does the HTML source look like? Figure 4.8 shows you.

Instead of showing all of the PHP code, the document displays, very simply, the results of the echo operation. PHP will only show what you tell it to show; the rest it either hides or performs another operation.

Rules

So we have now created our very own integer and displayed it on the screen. Let's go over some rules for the creation of variables. They have to abide by some naming guidelines.

Other than those listed here, the variable-naming rules are very lenient. Just be careful, and don't make any mistakes! An important thing to keep in mind is to make sure you keep your variable names descriptive. For example, do not use variable names such as $i. Instead, make it $numberCounter. You want to be able to tell what the variable does when you look at the source code a few weeks after you write it.

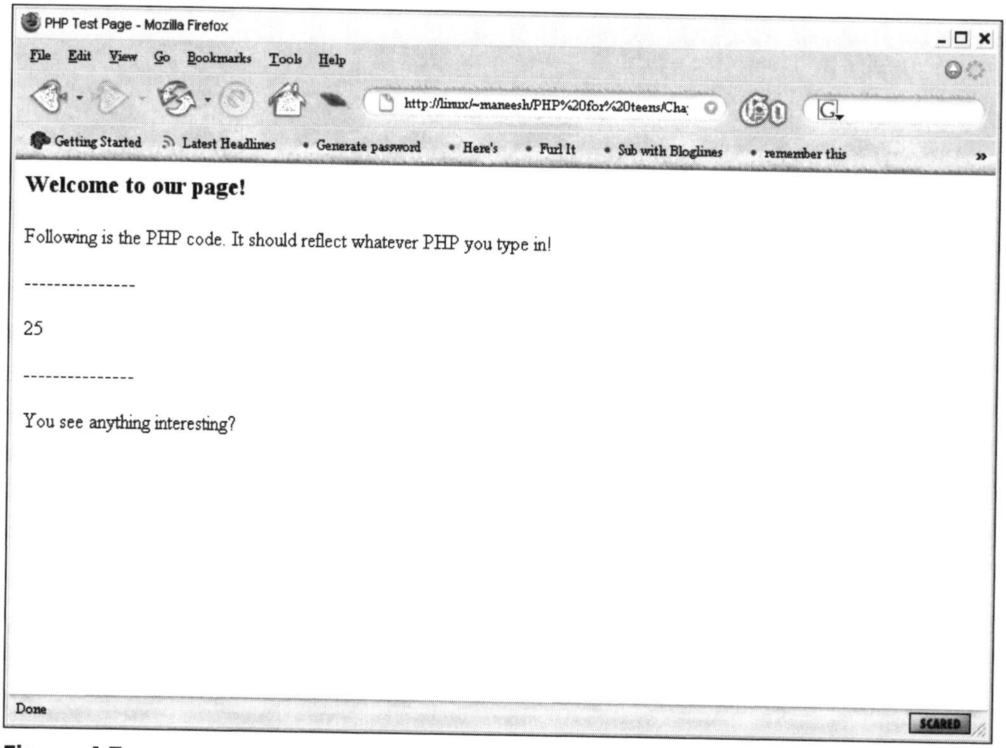

Figure 4.7
The `phpft04-02.php` file.

Start with Letter or Underscore

Variable names can only start with a letter or an underscore (_). After the first letter, a variable can be made up of letters, underscores, or numbers. Therefore, these variable names are both valid:

```
$newname
$_VariableForUse
```

Because it starts with a number, this variable is invalid:

```
$2variable
```

Mind Your Case

PHP is a *case-sensitive language*, meaning that capitalization matters in the variable names, statements, and other calls in your programs. `$Variable` is different than `$variable`. Be extra careful that you don't accidentally capitalize variables in your code when you don't want them to be capitalized.

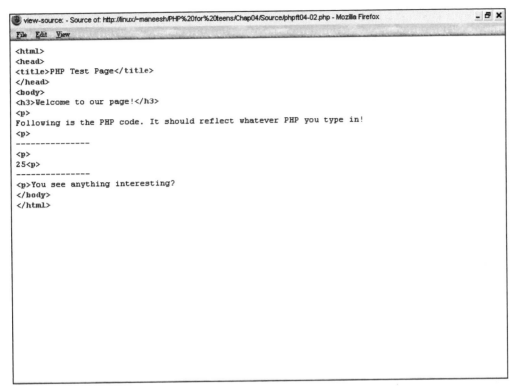

Figure 4.8
The phpft04-02.php source.

Functions and Parameters

Let's go back to that program we were just working on and see what we can do with some more variables. Remember how we talked about the different types of variables? There is a cool function in PHP called get_type(). This function returns a variable's type, so you can find out if it is a Boolean, a string, an integer, or something else.

What is a function? It is very similar to the echo language construct we used earlier. A *function* is a piece of centralized code that can be called from within your program and reused over and over again. It is basically a way to have PHP perform some actions on some data. There are predefined and self-written functions. I stick with predefined in this chapter.

You can send something called a *parameter* to many functions. The function then acts upon this parameter. In the case of get_type(), the parameter we pass is the variable whose type we want to know. Functions can also return a value, which

can be used for many purposes. Here, the return value is the name of the type that
the variable uses, such as integer or float.

Let's use get_type() in a program. We are going to add this function to the
program we created earlier. Let's create a bunch of variables of different types,
then see if the types were correctly identified by PHP. First create the variables:

```php
<?php
$integervar=25;
$booleanvar=TRUE;
$floatvar=314.13;
$stringvar="Hello, World!";
$nullvar=NULL;
```

Now echo out the variable types:

```php
echo "integervar: ".gettype($integervar);
echo "<br>booleanvar: ".gettype($booleanvar);
echo "<br>floatvar: ".gettype($floatvar);
echo "<br>stringvar: ".gettype($stringvar);
echo "<br>nullvar: " .gettype($nullvar);
?>
```

Putting it all into the HTML document, we get the following:

```html
<!DOCTYPE html PUBLIC "-//W3C//DTD XHTML 1.0 Strict//EN"
    "http://www.w3.org/TR/xhtml1/DTD/xhtml1-strict.dtd">
<html xmlns="http://www.w3.org/1999/xhtml" xml:lang="en" lang="en">
<head>
<title>PHP Test Page</title>
</head>
<body>
<h3>Welcome to our page!</h3>
<p>
Following is the PHP code. It should reflect whatever PHP you type in!
<p>
--------------
<p>

<?php
$integervar=25;
$booleanvar=TRUE;
$floatvar=314.13;
$stringvar="Hello, World!";
$nullvar=NULL;
```

```
echo "integervar: ".gettype($integervar);
echo "<br>booleanvar: ".gettype($booleanvar);
echo "<br>floatvar: ".gettype($floatvar);
echo "<br>stringvar: ".gettype($stringvar);
echo "<br>nullvar: " .gettype($nullvar);
?>
<p>
----------------

<p>You see anything interesting?
</body>
</html>
```

So how does this look? Well, check out Figure 4.9 to see.

Not bad at all, huh? We got the page working correctly! The only thing that looks a little weird is that the *float* variable is classified as a double, but both double and float are equivalent, so it is not a problem. Look at what source is generated in Figure 4.10. The source shows how PHP reinterprets the code to become just regular HTML.

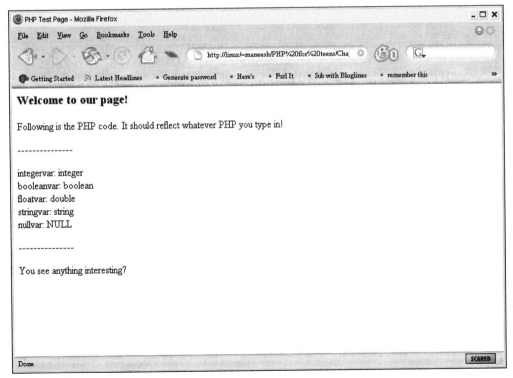

Figure 4.9
The `phpft04-03.php` file.

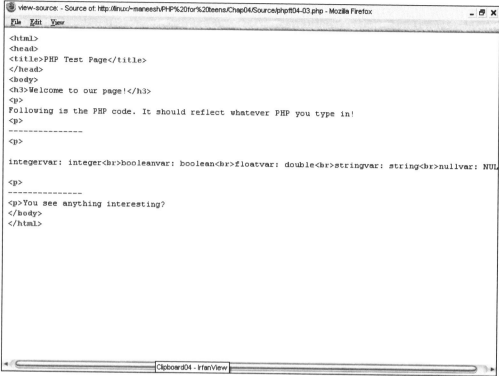

Figure 4.10
The `phpft04-03.php` source.

Now that I've gone over some basic variables, let me show you some other special types.

Predefined Variables and Arrays

PHP includes some predefined variables—those it designates. Some of these variables are created by the web server or sent by GET or POST forms (which I went over in Chapter 3). You can use these variables within your program for a lot of things. Before we move on, let's talk a little about the difference between GET and POST.

GET **Versus** POST

In all of your forms, you have the option of using GET or POST. Both are useful in different cases, so you should know the difference between the two. When using a GET form, all of the variable data are passed along in the URL's address bar. This means that you can look at the URL and see all the variables and their values. On the other hand, POST hides all the variables from the address bar—instead, it is transparently passed to the PHP program.

For example, say you had a page at www.something.com/page.php, which uses a GET form, and that the form passes the data to itself. After inputting the values and pressing submit, the address bar might look like the following:

```
http://www.something.com/page.php?first=value1&second=value2
```

In this case, there are two fields on the form: The first field has the name set to first, and the user entered in value1 in the textbox. The second field is called second and the value is value2. As you can see, all the data is passed along the address bar. This means that the user can manually change the values without even going through the form. POST, on the other hand, does not show the data in the URL address bar. After submitting the form, the address will look like this:

```
http://www.something.com/page.php
```

So why would you use one or the other? In some cases, it is important to secure data by not passing it in the address bar. For example, if the form is a log in, you don't want the password to be displayed in the address bar; you would use POST. Alternatively, if you want the user to be able to bookmark a page through a form, using GET allows that.

Arrays

To access the predefined variables, we have to use a variable array. *Arrays* are sets of variables that all have the same name, but are referenced by a specific number. Arrays look exactly like a normal variable, except it has a reference number attached to the end of the name. For example, while a normal variable might be called $name, an array of three names would look like this: $name[0], $name[1], $name[2]. In addition, arrays can use reference words rather than digits—for example, $name["first"] or $name["second"]. The number or word that you use to reference the variable in the array (such as first or 0) is called a *key*. You use the => operator to send the value into the key.

You can create your own arrays in a few ways. The easiest way is to simply define each individual item from the array. For example, to create a few variables of the array $name, we could do it like this:

```
$name[1] = "Maneesh";
```

```
$name[2] = "John";
$name[3] = "Smith";
```

There are some quicker ways. You can add values to the array at the same time you create it. This is done as follows:

```
$name = array(key => value, key=>value);
```

As you can see, you can designate any number of items in the array at the same time by using different values and keys. We could do this with our $name array as follows:

```
$name = array(1=>"Maneesh", 2 => "John", 3 => "Smith");
```

We now have an array that contains these three names. To print out Maneesh, for example, the value of $name[1], we would write this:

```
echo $name[1];
```

Predefined Variables

A lot of the predefined variables that PHP creates deal with forms, like the ones we created in Chapter 3. When you use a form, submit it with the method post or get. There are a few differences on these two, which we will go over in the next chapter, but when you use a form that submits, it transfers its data (such as a name or comments) through a method of either post or get.

When the page finishes submitting, it passes the data to the following page inside a predefined variable array. It will use either the $_GET or a $_POST array, depending on the method you used. To access the actual item, make the array's key the same as the name field of the part of the form you want.

This may sound a little complex, but it will make a little more sense if I show you an example. Let's create two pages: a form that asks for only a name and a page that displays the name. Because the first page is only a form, it can be named form.html, while the second requires PHP and therefore needs the extension .php. We will make it phpft04-04.php. (By the way, I go into much more depth on programs of this nature in the next chapter. This one is simply to show how to access a predefined array.)

A simple web page with a post form might look like the following. This is the text to the form.html file.

```
<!DOCTYPE html PUBLIC "-//W3C//DTD XHTML 1.0 Strict//EN"
    "http://www.w3.org/TR/xhtml1/DTD/xhtml1-strict.dtd">
<html xmlns="http://www.w3.org/1999/xhtml" xml:lang="en" lang="en">
<head>
<title>A sample PHP form</title>
</head>

<body>
<form action="phpft04-04.php" name="form" method="post">
Please enter your first name: <input type="text" name="firstName">
<br />
<input type="submit">
</form>
</body>
</html>
```

This is a very basic page that displays a small form and a submit button. It looks like Figure 4.11.

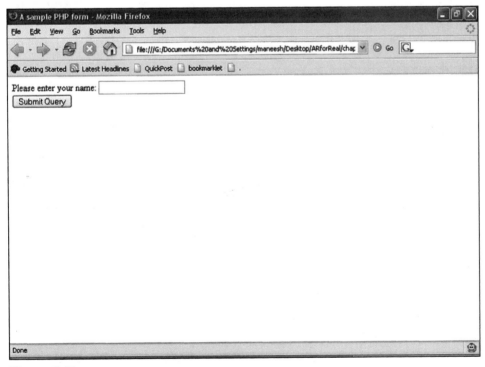

Figure 4.11
The form.html file.

Now you need a PHP page that takes the variable outside the form and displays it on the page. Notice that in the HTML document, the form uses the post method and the text field is called firstName. This is how the PHP document appears.

```
<!DOCTYPE html PUBLIC "-//W3C//DTD XHTML 1.0 Strict//EN"
    "http://www.w3.org/TR/xhtml1/DTD/xhtml1-strict.dtd">
<html xmlns="http://www.w3.org/1999/xhtml" xml:lang="en" lang="en">
<head>
<title>The results of the form using PHP</title>
</head>

<body>
<?php
//Echo out the first name of the userecho 'The name that you put into the previous
form was '.$_POST['firstName'];
?>
</body>

</html>
```

Figure 4.12
The php04-04.php file.

Table 4.2 Predefined Variable Arrays

Array	Description
$GLOBALS	References every global variable available; rarely used.
$_SERVER	Variables set by the server, such as the name of the file being used.
$_GET	Variables from a form that uses the GET method.
$_POST	Variables from a form that use the POST method.
$_REQUEST	A combination of the variables from $_GET, $_POST, and $_COOKIE.
$_COOKIE	Variables that are provided as cookies, which can be set.
$_FILES	Files that are uploaded via HTTP post.
$_ENV	PHP environment variables.
$_SESSION	Variables that are currently registered to script's session.

The echo line displays the text within the single quotation marks (') and then attaches that line to the variable $_POST['name'] using the dot operator (.), which joins a string to a variable. What is this crazy text that follows the //? Well actually, that is a comment. If you enter a //, anything that follows it on the same line is hidden from the program. This helps you remember what the program does when you look at it later. Comments are very important, so use them whenever you can! This page shows how you can use this predefined variable array to use forms. The page ends up looking like Figure 4.12.

You know all about how to use these arrays now; find out some more of the arrays that you can use. Check out Table 4.2.

These are the most common, but even some of these are rarely used. You don't need to know all about them, so I discuss them when they come up.

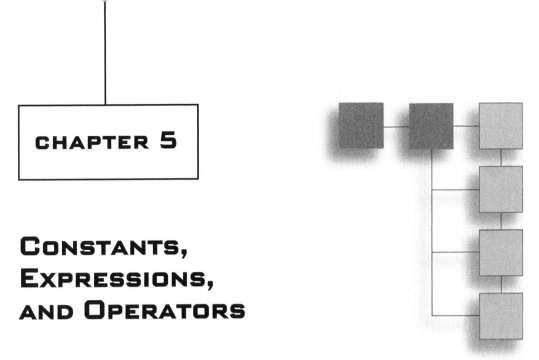

CHAPTER 5

CONSTANTS, EXPRESSIONS, AND OPERATORS

In this chapter, we are going to go over some of the language basics. You use constants, expressions, and operators in a lot of programs and web pages, so it is very important to learn all about them. Let's move forward and work with them. Ready?

Constants

Constants are an important concept to learn because they can make your programs a lot safer. Imagine a program that converts hours into days. You might have a `hoursPerDay` constant that always equals 24. You can define *constants*, but once they are defined they can never be redefined or undefined. Unlike variables, constants never change throughout the entire program. Use constants whenever, for instance, you have a value you want to multiply all inputs by or a known natural constant such as pi. Because the program cannot change the constant's value, it is guaranteed to work correctly.

You define constants differently than you do variables. With variables, you simply do something like this:

```
$variable = value;
```

You can change the value again just by doing something like this:

```
$variable = newvalue;
```

Makes sense, right? Well, with constants, it is a little different. Defining a constant requires the use of a function called define(). You need to pass along two parameters to the define() function for it to work. The first parameter is the name of the constant, and the second is the constant's value. The function is defined like this:

```
define("CONSTANTNAME", constantvalue);
```

Here are a few defined sample constants:

```
define("BOOLEANCONSTANT", TRUE);
define("INTEGERCONSTANT", 768);
define("FLOATCONSTANT", 469.12);
define("STRINGCONSTANT", "I am a string!");
```

Pretty cool, huh? I only defined these four types of constants (Boolean, integer, float, and string) because they are the only valid types of constants. Constants can be defined anywhere in your program and are accessible without regard to scope.

Another difference between constants and variables: When using a variable, you use a $ sign. For example, to print out a variable on the screen, you might do this:

```
echo $variablename;
```

However, constants are referred to simply by name; they do not need a symbol. To display a constant on the screen, you would probably do something like this:

```
echo CONSTANTNAME;
```

Constants are like variables in that they are case sensitive. Make sure you pay attention to their capitalization. You can capitalize all the letters (as I have been doing, simply for stylistic purposes) or you can choose all lowercase letters. However, whenever you reference your constants in the program, make sure that you use the correct capitalization scheme. For example, say you write a program that defines NAME as Smith, and the program echoes it on the screen. You need to echo it with the correct capitalization. What happens when we echo it incorrectly?

```
<?php

define("NAME","Smith");
echo name;

?>
```

There is an apparent error in this page. We created the constant to be named NAME. However, we displayed the variable name, which has not been created yet. Figure 5.1 shows you the results.

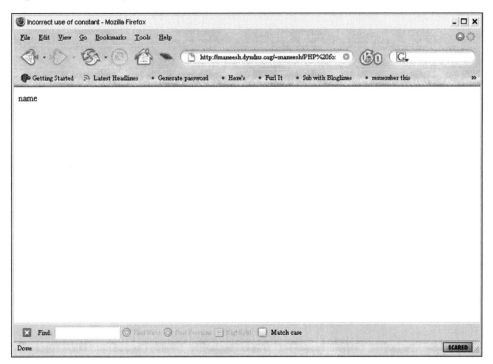

Figure 5.1
The phpft05-01.php incorrect constant file.

See how it displays name rather than the correct value? PHP assumes that if you have not created a constant for the value you echo, it should echo it as a string. Therefore, it converts NAME to name. Let's rewrite it so that it uses the correct capitalization and check out the results in Figure 5.2:

```php
<?php

define("NAME","Smith");
echo NAME;

?>
```

Operators

An *operator* is a helper in PHP that deals with one or more values and returns a different value. This may seem very vague, but operators are everywhere. Think about a math class. When you do basic addition, what are you doing? You are

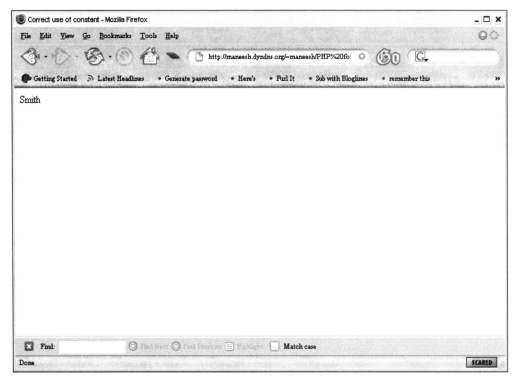

Figure 5.2
The `phpft05-02.php` correct constant file.

taking in two values (7 and 5, for example), adding them together (7 + 5), and receiving a different value (12). In this case, the plus sign is the operator causing the change.

Think about the `gettype()` function that we went over in Chapter 4. This function takes in a variable name and returns its type. This function is an operator because it takes in a value (the variable) and results in something different (a type). Sure, these two pieces of data may be different, but the function still acts upon it!

There are three classes of operators.

Note

Even though functions do act upon data, we generally don't think of functions as operators. We consider functions to be their own type of construction, and just deal with PHP default operators as operators.

Unary

A *unary* operator acts only upon one input. For example, the ++ operator increments a variable by 1. For example, assume you type the following:

```
$x = 10
$x++;
$echo $x;
```

You get the result 11.

Binary

Binary operators act upon two pieces of data. Think about the addition problem I just mentioned. There were two pieces of data: 5 and 7. Both of these, along with the operator ±, achieve a new result. Binary operators include arithmetic operators such as multiplication and division, as well as testing operators such as greater than or less than.

Ternary

There is only one *ternary* operator. This one is a little weird if you have never seen it before, and it is used a lot less than the binary operators, but it can be powerful when used correctly. The operator is called the ?: operator because it works with three sets of data. The first set comes before the question mark, and it is a test; for example, $x>$y determines whether $x is greater than $y.

- If the test is true, then the result is after the question mark (but before the colon).

- If the test is false, then the result is after the colon.

Before going into the rest of the operators, look at an example using the ternary operator. If you want to do the same test to check if $x is larger than $y, you might want to echo out the results. Take a look at the following PHP document, then check out Figure 5.3 to see the result:

```
<!DOCTYPE html PUBLIC "-//W3C//DTD XHTML 1.0 Strict//EN"
    "http://www.w3.org/TR/xhtml1/DTD/xhtml1-strict.dtd">
<html>
<head>
<meta http-equiv="content-type" content="text/html; charset=utf-8" />
<title>Using the ternary operator</title>
</head>
```

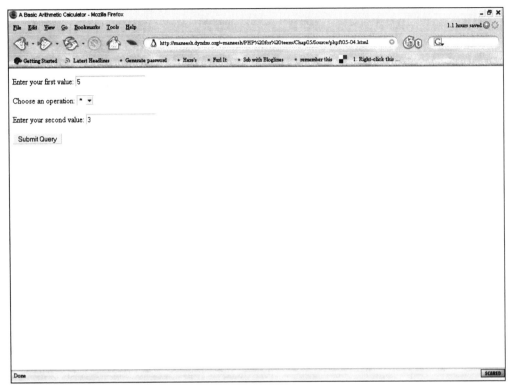

Figure 5.3
The `phpft05-03.php` ternary operator file.

```
<body>
<?php

$x = 7;
$y = 10;

//If x is greater than y, $ans = "greater", otherwise it equals "less"
$ans = ($x > $y) ? "greater" : "less";

//Print out the result
echo "<p>After the test, we have determined that $x is $ans than $y</p>";

?>
</body>

</html>
```

In this case, we gave variable values to $x and $y. We then used the ternary operator to give a value to the variable $ans, which could have the result of greater or less, depending on whether $x is greater than or less than $y. Let's take an in-depth look.

```
$ans = ($x > $y) ? "greater" : "less";
```

First, $ans is created and is left to the side to be assigned to the operation results. Next, the operator tests the expression ($x > $y). If this is true, then the first result is returned: greater. If the test is false, then the second result is returned: less. Because $ans is assigned to the result, it can only be either greater or less. In this example, $x was not greater than $y, so the result was false and $ans was less. We then plugged this value into an echo statement:

```
echo "After the test, we have determined that $x is $ans than $y";
```

This statement echoes the results. First, it writes out "After the test, we have determined that .". Then it writes out the value of $x, followed by is, displays the $ans value, and shows than $y". Because $ans can only be greater or less, it will make a valid sentence. By the way, if $x and $y are both equal to the same number, the program is blank. In a real program, you need to handle that event.

You might have noticed that I used a different scheme to write out the echo statement. Earlier, we used single quotes to echo out text; here I used double quotes. Check out the sidebar to find out why.

Why can I echo with double quotes or single quotes?

When using an echo command (or any command that requires quotation marks), consider whether you want to use single or double quotes. When writing out basic text, there is no difference. For example, echo 'Hello, World!' is identical to echo "Hello, World!". However, when you use variables or constants within an echo statement, double quotes and single quotes are very different. Double quotes allow you to place a variable directly into the string, referenced by a $ symbol; PHP substitutes the variable's value. However, with single quotes, the value is not substituted; instead, the page displays the quote's *name*. To use variables within single-quoted statements, you need to use the dot operator (.), ending the string with a single quote and using the dot operator to join a variable and the string.

Arithmetic Operators

Arithmetic operators are the most common. Most are basically the same ones you have known your entire life: addition, subtraction, multiplication, and division. Arithmetic operators act just like you would expect them to when you do something like what you see in Table 5.1.

Table 5.1 Arithmetic Operators

Task	Symbol	Example
Add two numbers	Addition (+)	$sum = $a + $b
Subtract two numbers	Subtraction (-)	$different = $a - $b
Multiply two numbers	Asterisk (*)	$product = $a * $b
Divide two numbers	Forward slash (/)	$quotient = $a / $b
Retrieve a negative number	Subtraction (-)	$negative = - $a
Retrieve a division remainder	Percentage (%)	$remainder = $a % $b?

The last two might be new to you. The *negative operator* returns the number's negative value. For example, using the negative operator on 7 would return -7. This operator is a unary operator, meaning it only works on one input. The last arithmetic operator is called the *modulus operator*. It works in the same way as any of the binary operators. For instance, 7%7 would return 0 because there is no remainder in a 7/7 division problem. In 9%7, the answer is 2, because there is a remainder. Modulus is awesome for checking some specific things, such as if a number is even or odd. 6%2 is 0, meaning the number (6) is even, and 5%2 is odd (and it is equal to 1), meaning that 5 is odd. If you are checking remainders, modulus is excellent for that purpose.

Let's put all these arithmetic operators into a program. We will use a basic calculator form. Here is the form that we created to do this job. You can find it on the CD as `phpft05-04.html`:

```
<!DOCTYPE html PUBLIC "-//W3C//DTD XHTML 1.0 Strict//EN"
    "http://www.w3.org/TR/xhtml1/DTD/xhtml1-strict.dtd">

<html>

<head>
<title>A Basic Arithmetic Calculator</title>
</head>

<body>
<form name="calculator" method="get" action="phpft05-04.php">
<p>
Enter your first value:
<input type="text" name="first" />
<p>Choose an operation:
<select name="operation">
```

```
<option value="+">+
<option value="-">-
<option value="*">*
<option value="/">/
<option value="%">%

</select>

<p>
Enter your second value:
<input type="text" name="second" />
<p>
<input type="submit" >
</form>

</body>

</html>
```

This looks like Figure 5.4, where I substituted some sample values.

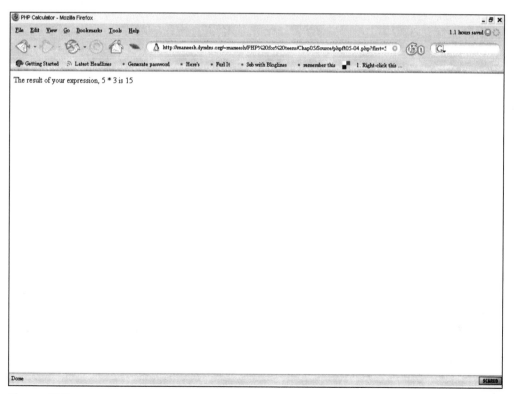

Figure 5.4
The phpft05-03.html calculator form file.

As you can see, this creates a sample form which sends its data through the GET method to a PHP file. The form code also creates a cool drop-down box, pictured in Figure 5.5.

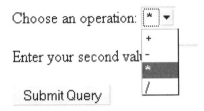

Figure 5.5
A drop-down box.

The following <select> HTML element makes the drop-down box show up:

```
<select name="operation">

<option value="+">+
<option value="-">-
<option value="*">*
<option value="/">/
<option value="%">%

</select>
```

Each option has a value, which you set. When using PHP, the selected option is passed into the $_GET[] or $_POST[] variable, just as if the user had entered the value in a textbox. Therefore, if the user selects /, the $_GET['operation'] variable will be equal to /.

Now, the PHP document is a little more complex than anything we have seen so far. Check out the code:

```
<!DOCTYPE html PUBLIC "-//W3C//DTD XHTML 1.0 Strict//EN"
    "http://www.w3.org/TR/xhtml1/DTD/xhtml1-strict.dtd">
<html>
<head>
<title>PHP Calculator</title>
</head>

<body>
<?php
```

```php
//put form variables in standard variables
$a = $_GET['first'];
$b = $_GET['second'];
$op = $_GET['operation'];

echo "The result of your expression, $a $op $b is ";

//Check the operation and deal with the result correctly
if($op=='+')
{
  echo $a + $b;
}

if($op=='-')
{
  echo $a - $b;
}

if($op=='*')
{
  echo $a * $b;
}

if($op=='/')
{
  echo $a/$b;
}

if ($op=='%')
{
  echo $a%$b;
}

?>
</body>

</html>
```

That's pretty crazy, huh? Check out the results in Figure 5.6.

This page introduces you to something new: conditional statements. For this page, you have to do something different depending on what operator the user chooses. Because of this, we use the if statements you see in the preceding code. Basically, the statement tests whether something is true. This test is within the

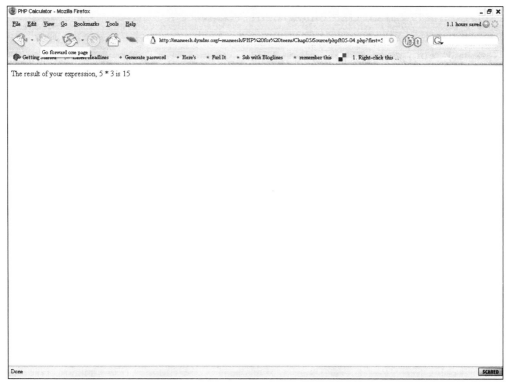

Figure 5.6
The `phpft05-04.php` file.

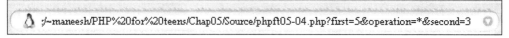

Figure 5.7
The address bar using the `GET` method.

parentheses after the word if. If the test is true, then whatever is in the curly braces (`'{' '}'`) occurs. If not, then the statement doesn't occur. (I go over this in depth in the next part, when I talk about conditional statements. I wanted to introduce this here because if statements are everywhere and it helps to understand what they do, even if you can't write them yourself yet.)

One other thing to notice in this page: This is the first time we used the `GET` method rather than `POST`. Take a look at the address bar after filling out the form and pressing submit. Figure 5.7 shows you what mine says.

You see the tricky part? It actually encodes the variables *within* the address bar. This means that you can see the variables you passed along with the form just by

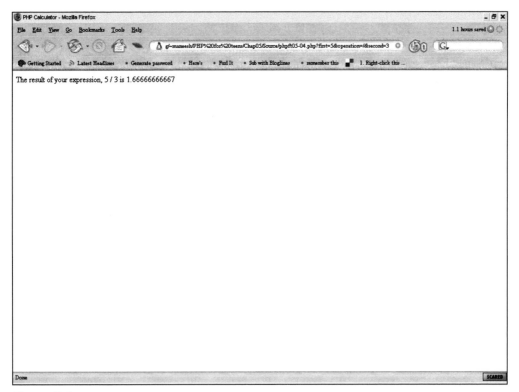

Figure 5.8
Changing the variables in a GET form.

looking at the URL. This also means that you can bookmark the results, and they will continue to show the correct results. With the POST method, you lose the form results each time. Also, Figure 5.8 shows what happens when I change the address bar to pass / rather than * for the operator. You can see here that it actually changes the page results.

Using GET is great for pages where you want a visitor to be able to return. Since the data is stored in the URL, the user can easily bookmark the page with the correctly inputted information and access the interpreted data without submitting the form each time. However, GET has some drawbacks:

- There is a URL-length limit that prevents you from having unlimited variables in the page.

- Information is not secure. When passing secure information, such as a password, it is much better to use POST so that the sensitive data is not shown in the address bar.

Table 5.2 Comparison Operators

Task	Symbol	Example
Return true if values are equal.	Equal (=)	$a == $b
Return true if values are equal and the same type.	Identical (==)	$a == $b
Return true if the values are not equal.	Not equal (<>)	$a != $b or $a <> $b
Return true if the values are unequal or are different types.	Not identical (!==)	$a !== $b
Return true if the first value is less than the second.	Less than (<)	$a < $b
Return true if the first value is larger than the second.	Greater than (>)	$a > $b
Return true if the first value is less than or equal to the second.	Less than or equal to (<=)	$a <= $b
Return true if the first value is greater than or equal to the second.	Greater than or equal to (>=)	$a >= $b

Comparison Operators

Take a look at the PHP document. See how the if statements test for equality using the == operator? That's a comparison operator. *Comparison operators* allow you to test two values against each other, and if they relate correctly, the test returns true. If the relationship specified by the test is incorrect, the return value is false. All comparison operators are binary, meaning they take two values in for input. Take a look at Table 5.2 for all of them.

These operators can be used within any type of flow-control system, such as if tests or, as you learn later, switch tests. They are great tools for checking values.

Note

Keep in mind that the equality operator (==) is different than the assignment operator (=). The assignment operator changes the variable on the left to have a new value, while the equality variable tests for equality and returns a 1 if true.

Logical Operators

Logical operators are used when two or more comparisons are needed for a test. For example, you would use a logical operator if you needed to determine that $number is greater than 7 and also less than 10. With logical operators, you can do this and execute a statement only if $number is equal to 8 or 9. Table 5.3 lists the logical operators. For this table, $a and $b are comparisons, so in the preceding example, $a would be $number > 7 and $b would be $number < 10.

Table 5.3 Logical Operators

Task	Symbol	Example
Return true if both comparisons are true.	and	$a and $b
Return true if either comparison is true or both comparisons are true.	or	$a or $b
Return true if either comparison is true, but not both.	xor	$a xor $b
Return true is the comparison is not true.	!	!$a
Return true if both comparisons are true.	&&	$a && $b
Return true if either comparison is true or both comparisons are true.	||	$a || $b

Precedence can be an issue with logical operators. Be careful to always use parentheses. Here's an example: Pretend that you have three different statements—A, B, and C. Here are two different tests:

- (A and B) or C

- A and (B or C)

The test in the parentheses is always executed first.

Other Operators

A few more operators don't really fit into the other categories, but you should know them because they are useful.

Assignment

You know this one already, because you used it to create a variable. This operator uses the = symbol, and it assigns a value to a variable. For example, the following is an assignment operation:

$x = 13;

The variable $x has the value 13. This assignment operation returns the value of the assignment, so if you set a new variable equal to the result of this operation, it is also equal to 13.

Incrementing and Decrementing

The operators add 1 to the value of an integer, meaning they are all unary. Look at the following samples of incrementing (the first two) and decrementing operators (the last two):

```
$a++
$++a
$a--
$--a
```

The value of each number increases by 1 when using the ++ operator and decreases by 1 when using the -- operator. For example, look at the following:

```
$a = 10;
$a++;
echo $a;
$a--;
echo $a;
```

The variable $a is given a starting value of 10. It is then incremented, and the first echo statement shows the variable as having a value of 11. The second echo statement shows $a as having the value of 10, because the -- operation decrements it.

Note

You might be wondering why both operators can be attached to either the beginning or the end of the variable name. Attaching it to the front versus the back has similar results, but there is one important difference: When attaching the operator to the front, the variable is incremented by 1, and then the new value is returned. When the operator is attached to the back, the old value of the operator is returned, and *then* the variable is incremented by 1. For example, look at the following code:

```
$a=10;
echo $a++;
$a=10;
echo ++$a;
```

The first echo statement will show the variable as being equal to 10, but immediately after the echo, the variable becomes 11. On the second echo statement, the variable becomes 11 and then the variable is echoed.

String Dot Operator and Dot Assignment

The string dot operator attaches different parts of strings together to form one big string. Take a look at the following code:

```
$firstpart = "Welcome to ";
$secondpart= "my web site. ";
$fullstring = $firstpart . $secondpart;
```

$fullstring now contains the value "Welcome to my web site." The dot operator joins the two parts of the string.

The dot assignment operator (.=) appends a new string to the end of the first string. For example, the following code puts in "Welcome to my web site.":

```
$text = "Welcome to ";
$text .= "my web site.";
```

Expressions

Expressions are basically the most important element of PHP. In essence, anything that you write in PHP, anything that has a value, is considered an *expression*. If you create a statement that does something, it is generally an expression.

A very simple example of an expression—creating and assigning a variable—might look something like this:

```
$variablename = "value";
```

This creates a variable called variablename that is assigned to some value. Because "value" is a string, the variable $variablename will also be a string. See the semicolon at the end? That marks the end of a statement.

What is the difference between a statement and an expression?

Statements and expressions are both very common and very important. All statements are expressions, but not all expressions are statements. An expression is basically anything that has a value within a web page, such as a test or an assignment. A statement is something that forces something to be done, such as calling a function or an assignment. As you can see, an assignment is also clearly an expression. You can easily differentiate statements and expressions by looking at them—generally, statements end with a semicolon.

Expressions produce a value, which means that each expression returns a result. Let's take a simple integer assignment:

```
$intvar = 15;
```

You might see two parts to this expression: the value 15 and the assignment to $intvar. However, there is also one more step—the result of the actual assignment itself. This action returns a value. The value returned from an assignment is simply the value of the newly defined variable.

Let's look at an example of this. What happens if we assign a new variable to the value of the assignment?

```
$secondvar = ($firstvar = 15);
```

`$secondvar` will now have a result of 15, as will `$firstvar`. Both variables get the same result. This example shows what expressions are all about. You will need to use a mix of pure expressions and statements in your web pages to get the results you are looking for, and many times you will need to use compounds statements.

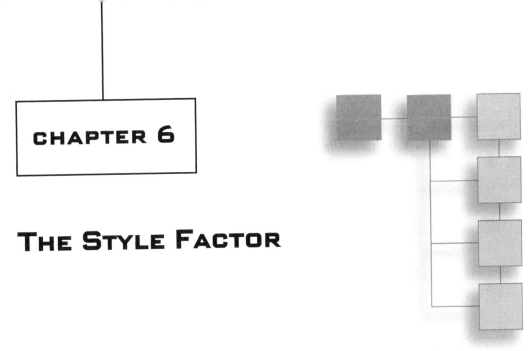

CHAPTER 6

THE STYLE FACTOR

This is the last chapter of the first part! Thus far, we've learned a lot about PHP programming, including designing a web page and forms, using variables and operators, and communicating with expressions in our web pages. All of these items are very important in PHP programming, but there is one part we have neglected to talk about so far: style. I use the word *style* in the sense of cleanliness and orderliness of your code. Whenever you develop a web page, you are going to have to write some code. This code, whether it is in HTML or PHP, can get rather large and ugly, so it is very important that you keep some structure within it.

No matter in what language you are writing your programs, your code style can become a big concern. Take the time to develop a structure. It will help make your code easier to understand.

Why Style?

You might be wondering why it even matters how organized or neat your code. After all, you are the only one who looks at it, right? It shouldn't matter whether your code is commented or easy to understand—right?

Wrong. Absolutely wrong. Many times I have written code for a game or project, and when I looked it over again three months later, I had no idea how the code worked. Even worse, sometimes I had errors in the code that I could not fix. If I had spent just a few more minutes making it neater or more organized, my efficiency would have been hundreds of times better. Instead, I wasted hours simply trying to catch an error (or even simply figure out what was going on). I once even read about a programmer who spent 30 minutes looking at a section of code asking, "Who is this idiot and what is he doing?" He later found out that it was his own work.

How can you achieve style? Take a look at the web page we designed:

```
<html><head><title>Quick Sample Page</title>
</head><body><h3>Welcome to our page!</h3>
<p>Hello,
    World!
</p>
<p><b>I am some bolded text</b>,
<i>I am some italicized
text</i>, <u>and I am some underlined text</u>. <u><i>I am both underlined and
italicized.</i></u>
</body>
</html>
```

This code is badly spaced, poorly organized, and does not flow. However, even though it looks poorly organized in code, check out how it looks on the screen in Figure 6.1.

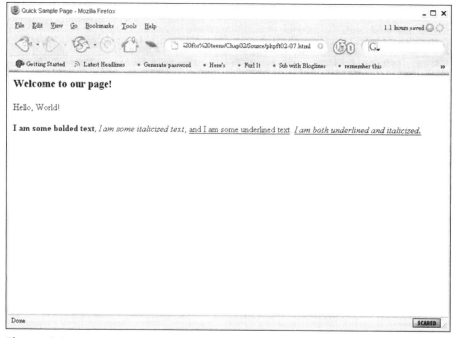

Figure 6.1
The unorganized `phpft06-01.html` file.

Now look at it spaced a little nicer:

```
<html>
<head>
    <title>Quick Sample Page</title>
</head>

<body>
    <h3>Welcome to our page!</h3>
    <p>
            Hello, World!
    </p>
    <p>
        <b>I am some bolded text</b>,
        <i>I am some italicized text</i>,
        <u>and I am some underlined text</u>.
        <u><i>I am both underlined and italicized.</i></u>
    </p>

</body>
</html>
```

A lot easier on the eyes this time, huh? You can see in Figure 6.2 that it looks exactly the same. That is because HTML and PHP don't care about how many spaces or tabs you put into your document—they remove all the white space before displaying the file on the screen. Because of this, it's a lot better to make easy to read in the first place.

This is the same with PHP. The following two samples of code are identical:

Example 1:

```
<?php$a = $_GET['first'];
$b = $_GET['second']; $op = $_GET['operation']; echo "The result of your
  expression, $a $op $b is ";
if($op=='+')
{echo $a + $b; }if($op=='-'){
echo $a - $b; }if($op=='*') {echo $a * $b;
}if($op=='/'){echo $a/$b;}

if ($op=='%'){
echo $a%$b;}?>
```

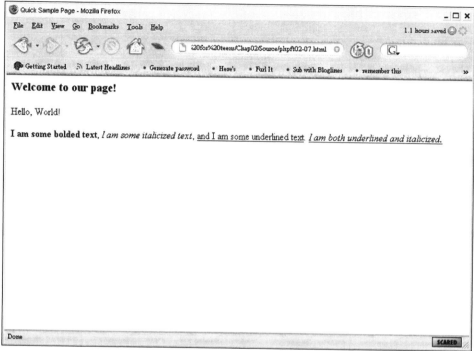

Figure 6.2
The organized phpft06-01.html file.

Example 2:

```php
<?php

$a = $_GET['first'];
$b = $_GET['second'];
$op = $_GET['operation'];

echo "The result of your expression, $a $op $b is ";
if($op=='+')
{
    echo $a + $b;
}

if($op=='-')
{
    echo $a - $b;
}

if($op=='*')
{
```

```
    echo $a * $b;
}

if($op=='/')
{
    echo $a/$b;
}

if ($op=='%')
{
    echo $a%$b;
}

?>
```

Isn't the second one so much nicer?

How to Style

There are millions of different style methods, but the most important part is that you stay consistent. You must follow a pattern. If you stray, put your pattern into words and print it—laminate it if you must. Again, the most important part is staying consistent.

What does this mean? You can choose to make all of your variables start with `var`, so that, for instance, a variable that contains a name is called `$varname`. Heck, you could even make it called `$afbkajfbkaname`, as long as you stay so consistent that your address variable is called `$afbkajfbkaaddress`. One popular way of keeping track of your variables is to preface each name with the type of variable it is. For example, a string called `$strFirstName` and an integer called `$intAge`.

Let me share some conventions that I follow for my own style. You don't have to follow what I say, but these are good general guidelines that will help you to find your own style.

Capitalization

I leave all of my variables lowercased. You will see variables like the following in my code:

```
$name
$homeaddress
$age
```

Take a look at that second example, $homeaddress. Notice that it is two words. I like to usually keep them both lowercase, and I can easily tell what it means. However, some people prefer to split up words in a variable with capital letters:

```
$homeAddress
$HomeAddress
```

I—and just about everyone else—capitalize all of my constants. Remember, constants are designated using the define() function.

```
TIME
CONVERSION
EMAILADDRESS
```

If you want to designate two words in a different way, you can use an underscore (_).

I use underscores for multiple-word functions. This makes it a little easier on the eyes. I go over functions in Chapter 9, so you should learn how to style them as well.

```
change_address()
build_model()
buy()
```

Underscores

One good way to organize your documents is to tab your tags and code. If you are using several tags in an HTML document, you can space them out nicely:

```
<body>
    <p>
        <b>I am bold!</b>
    </p>
</body>
```

If you do this, you can tell at a glance what tags refer to a piece of code.

Comments

Another important part of organization is understanding the use of comments. When you write a program, it all makes sense to you at the time. You know exactly why you wrote everything and how each piece of code does what it does. This won't always be the case, however. In only a few weeks, you may forget everything about how the program works.

Comments allow you to add text that the web server throws away; they make no difference on the outcome of the program. They *will* make a difference when you need to look at it only a few months later.

You should use comments in these places:

- At the beginning of every program

- At the beginning of any large section of code

- Just before any piece of code that other readers might not understand

- Throughout the program to help the reader understand its purpose and goal

There are three methods of adding comments: C, C++, and Perl. All are named after the programming languages in which they were introduced.

C Method

The C method allows you to comment out as much code as you want, spanning multiple lines. It does not take into account any line breaks. To use the C method, you enclose whatever you want commented by /* and */. For example, look at the following:

```
echo "I will be printed";
/* echo "I won't be printed";
Neither will I. */
```

As you can see, anything within the /* and */ marks is ignored.

C++ Method

The C++ method is a little different. This comments out anything on the same line, starting with the // symbol and ending with the new line. Look at the following example:

```
echo "I will be printed"; // I won't be printed, because of comments
echo "however, I will be printed, because this is a new line.";
```

Perl Method

The Perl method is exactly the same as the C++ method, except it uses a # sign:

```
echo "I will be printed"; # I won't be printed, because of comments
echo "however, I will be printed, because this is a new line."
```

The last thing we are going to do in this chapter is take that earlier code segment and add comments. Check it out:

```php
<?php

//Create three variables that take in the GET form data
$a = $_GET['first']; //This is the first operand
$b = $_GET['second']; //This is the second operand
$op = $_GET['operation']; //This is the operation to be preformed

//Write out introduction text to the screen
echo "The result of your expression, $a $op $b is ";

//If an addition problem, echo out an addition answer.
if($op=='+')
{
    echo $a + $b;
}

//If a subtraction problem, echo out a subtraction answer.
if($op=='-')
{
    echo $a - $b;
}

//If an multiplication problem, echo out a multiplication answer.
if($op=='*')
{
    echo $a * $b;
}

//If a division problem, echo out a division answer.
if($op=='/')
{
    echo $a/$b;
}

//If a modulus problem, echo out a modulus answer.
if ($op=='%')
{
    echo $a%$b;
}

?>
```

Easier to read and understand, huh?

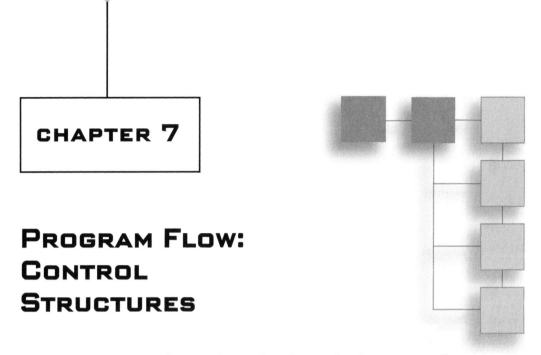

CHAPTER 7

PROGRAM FLOW: CONTROL STRUCTURES

You are going to use what you learned earlier to develop some really cool pages and PHP programs. Control structures are part of that, taking a comparison statement and performing a comparison. If the comparison is true, special statements are executed. If the comparison is false, the statements are skipped.

In this chapter, where I go over loops and branching structures, you learn ways to make your programs interactive and how to get PHP to act upon data and perform different actions depending on input.

Branching Structures

Control structures include *branching structures,* which allow your program to make all these things:

- if. . .then decisions

- *Loops,* which let you execute some code repeatedly

- Functions that put specialized code into their own separate section

When you run a program, you expect it to go from beginning to end. Usually, the program displays everything that is in the code, putting each section one after another. When you write an HTML page, every part of the page is displayed in the same order as it is defined in the source. However, you might want to change that flow. You might need to perform a different action because some special event occurs. PHP offers a way to do this with branching structures.

if

The easiest way is to use the if branching structure. A basic backbone looks like the following:

```
if (condition is true)
{
//execute statements
}
```

You obviously need to replace the comparison with a condition test. Condition tests are done using the comparison operators, such as <, >, !=, and so on. Take a look at Chapter 5 to see the comparison methods.

We will create a page that allows a user to enter two numbers, and we use PHP to compare the two numbers and say which is bigger. First, let's take a look at the form that would do this. We are going to use the GET submit method.

```
<html>

<head>
<title>Comparing two numbers</title>
</head>

<body>

<form name="compare" action="phpft07-01.php" method="get">

      Enter your first number: <input type="text" name="firstnumber">
      <br />Enter your second number: <input type="text" name="secondnumber">
      <br /><br /><input type="submit">
</form>

</body>

</html>
```

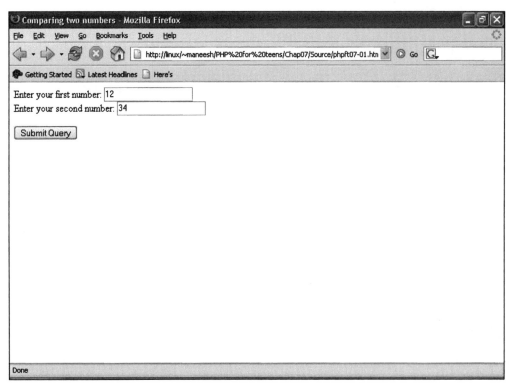

Figure 7.1
The phpft07-01.html form file.

This page ends up looking like Figure 7.1. I added the numbers into the textbox after opening the page.

Now look at the PHP page:

```
<html>

<head>
<title>Comparison of two numbers</title>
</head>
<body>
<?php

$a = $_GET['firstnumber'];
$b = $_GET['secondnumber'];

echo "Your first number was $a.";
echo "<br>Your second number was $b.";
```

```
echo "<p>";

if ($a > $b)
{
    echo "Your first number ($a) is greater than your second number ($b).";
}

if ($a < $b)
{
    echo "Your second number ($b) is greater than your first number ($a).";
}
?>

</body>
</html>
```

You see how this page works? Figure 7.2 shows what it looks like.

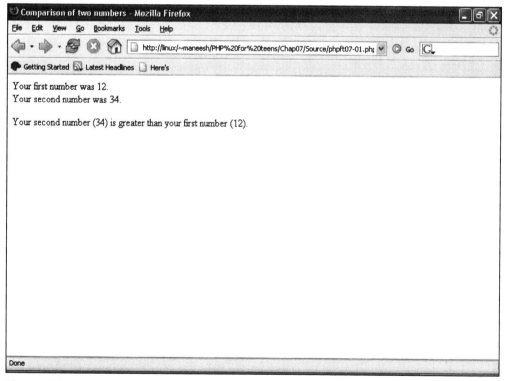

Figure 7.2
The `phpft07-01.php` results file.

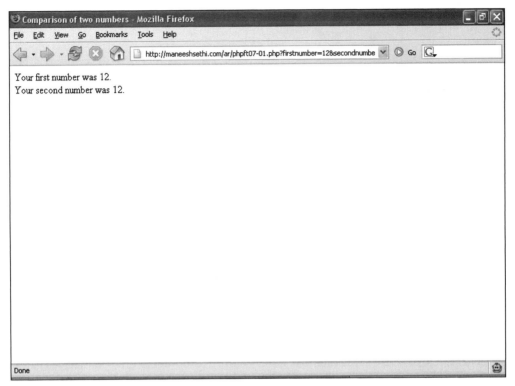

Figure 7.3
The form with equal values.

A couple if statements work together to determine whether the first number is larger than the second or vice versa. If the first one is greater, that is echoed, and if the second is greater than the first, the correct result is echoed. However, what happens if the numbers are equal? Check it out in Figure 7.3.

If the numbers are equal, nothing happens! We did not set up the program to do anything if this situation occurs. We obviously need to fix this.

else

Let me show you a new control structure that works tightly with the one you already know: else. When you join an if structure to an else structure, one of the two statements will be executed. If the comparison test is true, the if statements are executed, and if the test is false, the else statements are executed.

Look at a generalized else structure:

```
if (comparison is true)
{
//execute statements
}
else
{
//execute other statements
}
```

Let's try putting this into our file, with phpft07-02.php. (I copied over the HTML file for the CD as well, with the only change being the form action.)

```
if ($a > $b)
{
    echo "Your first number ($a) is greater than your second number ($b).";
}
else
{
    echo "Both your first number ($a) and your second number ($b) are equal!.";
}
if($a < $b)
{
    echo "Your second number ($b) is greater than your first number ($a).";
}
else
{
    echo "Both your first number ($a) and your second number ($b) are equal!.";
}
```

This makes sense, right? If the tests are false, it echoes out that the numbers are equal. However, we just created a couple of big problems. Try to see if you can find them, then check out Figure 7.4. Now it should be easier to spot the problem within the code.

You see here that it actually gives two results! The code is going through both structures. For the first structure, it checks to see if $a is greater than $b. This is not true, so it executes the else statements. Therefore, the first text written is that the two numbers are equal. Next, the code goes to the second if statement, where it determines that $a is indeed bigger than $b. Because the if control structure rings true, it executes the if statements and says that the second number is bigger than the first one.

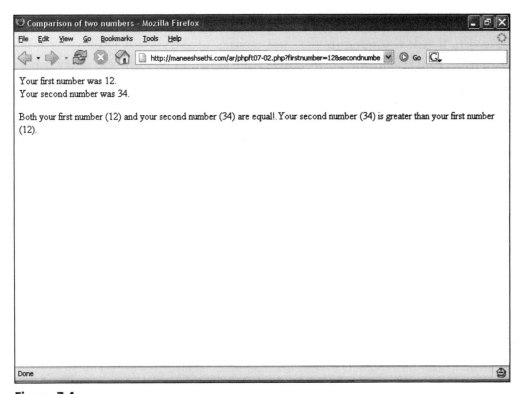

Figure 7.4
Using `phpft07-02.php` with some errors.

Before we move on, let's see what happens when you put in two equal numbers. The result is Figure 7.5.

Here, you can see that neither the first `if` or second structure is true. Because of this, both execute their second statements, ending up with two comments saying that the numbers are equal. We need to fix this so it only shows once and doesn't give the wrong answer every time.

elseif

We need to figure out a way to put `if` statements together so we can use the `else` command and not have to execute the same code twice. Fortunately, PHP provides a control structure called `elseif`, which is very similar to `if`. It is part of an `if` structure and only executes on two conditions: First, the `if` test needs to fail and second, its own `elseif` test needs to succeed. Check out the basic structure:

```
if (comparison is true)
{
//execute statements
}
```

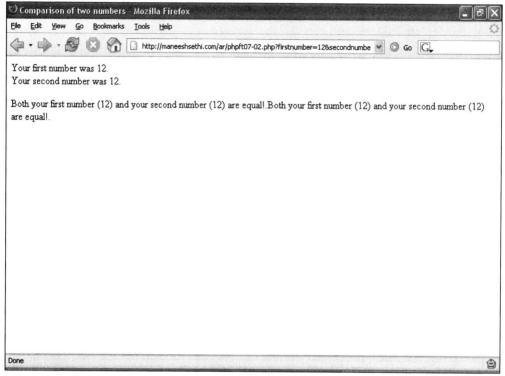

Figure 7.5
Using `phpft07-02.php` with equal numbers.

```
elseif (different comparison is true)
{
//execute other statements
}
```

You can add an `else` section to this control structure as well, which only executes if both the `if` and the `elseif` sections fail. Let's put the two `if` sections together on the page and add the `else`. This allows us to finally have a well-designed structure that gives no errors.

```
if ($a > $b)
{
    echo "Your first number ($a) is greater than your second number ($b).";
}
elseif ($a < $b)
{
echo "Your second number ($b) is greater than your first number ($a).";
}
```

```
else
{
echo "Both your first number ($a) and your second number ($b) are equal!.";
}
```

This structure can have only three possibilities. $a could be bigger than $b, $b could be bigger than $a, or they could be equal. However, only one of the three echo statements will be executed.

Caution

Take note that this page only deals with integers. If you enter a string rather than a number, you might get some erratic results.

Note

One other branching structure is the ternary structure, which is very similar to if. . .else. You can see some more examples with the ternary operator in Chapter 5.

switch

switch is excellent at comparing one variable to several possible values. switch only works when checking to see if an input is exactly the same as a value; you cannot run comparison tests on it. This is a great way to compare a variable against several different known values to see if something occurs. For example, you can see if $a equals 0 or a, but you cannot use switch to see if $a is greater than $b. The following is the generalized structure for a switch statement:

```
switch($variable)
{
    case 0:
        //execute statements
        break;
    case 1:
        //execute statements
        break;
    default:
        //execute statements only if none of the cases fit
        break;
}
```

Let's quickly recreate a program we did earlier. Remember when I introduced if control structures while designing the calculator? Let's go back to that and use switch instead of if. The HTML file is the same, except the action attribute has changed; the PHP file has changed. Check out what it now looks like. This file is phpft07-04.php on the CD. Figure 7.6 shows you what the form page looks like.

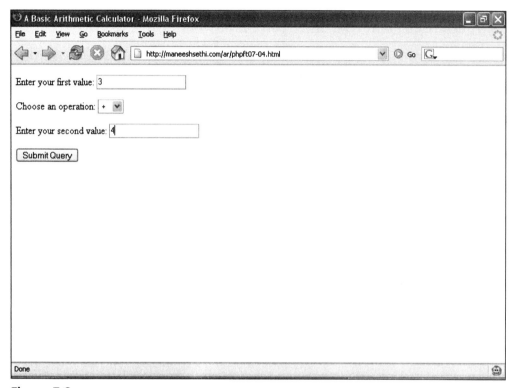

Figure 7.6
The phpft07-04.html form file.

```php
<?php

//Put $_GET variables into our own variables
$a = $_GET['first'];
$b = $_GET['second'];
$op = $_GET['operation'];

echo "The result of your expression, $a $op $b is ";
//Echo out the result of the chosen operation
switch ($op)
{

case '+':
        echo $a + $b;
        break;
```

```
case '-':
        echo $a - $b;
        break;

case '*':
        echo $a * $b;
        break;

case '/':
        echo $a/$b;
        break;

case '%':
        echo $a%$b;
        break;

default:
        echo "Warning: Operation Not Valid";
        break;

}

?>
```

This replaces it all with switch, including a default value just in case the user enters something that gives a big error. One result might look like Figure 7.7.

You might be wondering what the break statements do. switch is designed so that the execution of one of the commands will flood into another one. So, for example, if we removed the breaks and did an addition problem on our calculator, we would get six results: the addition, the subtraction, the multiplication, the division, the modulus, and the default echo. break stops this by exiting directly out of the switch structure. As a general rule, always use a break after each case unless there is an overbearing reason not to do so.

It's important to note that I included a default case for the switch statement, even though it appears impossible for the operation to ever be anything other than the given choices. However, you should always include a default clause for your switch statement. What if the form is a GET form and the user changes the operation through the URL? Other things can come up that may confuse your program, so it is always better to be safe and simply use a default clause.

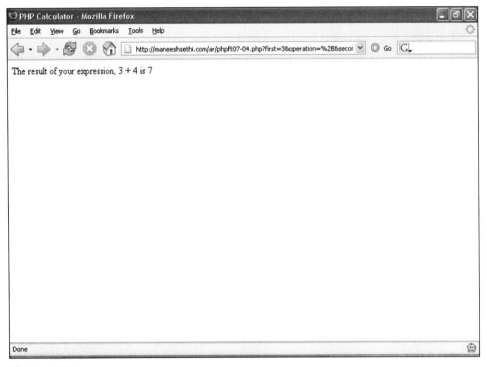

Figure 7.7
The `phpft07-04.php` file.

Loops

Sometimes, while designing a program, you need to execute a set of statements repeatedly. You might need to display an entire set of data with hundreds of elements or list all numbers from 1 to 100. Fortunately, PHP offers *loops,* which allow you to execute a set of statements as many times as needed. There are several different types of loops. Each type has strengths and weaknesses. You most often find loops with arrays, which I go over in Chapter 10.

while

Let's start off with the most common loop: `while`. Using the `while` loop, you execute the statements as long as a certain condition is true. Remember the three stages of the `while` loop:

- Initialization outside the loop, which ensures the loop executes at least once

- Condition inside the `while` statement

- Code inside the loop, which causes it to end

Let's look at the structure:

```
while (condition is true)
{
    //execute repeated statements
} //end of loop
```

You can enter whatever statements you want executed.

Caution

Be careful—you don't want to accidentally create a loop that is always true. If the statement inside the condition test is never false, the loop will execute forever. This could occur if you write something like while (1==1) or even while(1), because any non-zero number is always considered true. A common error is to check some condition that never occurs, such as while ($x!=7), when the variable $x never actually becomes 7. If you do this, the loop continues forever and the page never loads correctly.

Let's create a simple program: a counter that counts from 1 to 10 and then displays the digits on the screen. This file is phpft07-05.php on the CD and results in a page that looks like Figure 7.8.

```
<html>
<head>
<title>A counter from 1 to 10 using while</title>
</head>

<body>

<?php

//give starting value to counter
$counter=1;

//increment counter from 1 to 10
while ($counter<=10)
{
    echo "$counter<br />";
    $counter++;
}

?>
</body>
</html>
```

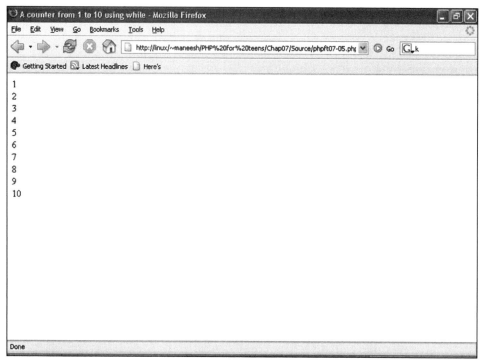

Figure 7.8
The `phpft07-05.php` file.

As you can see, this program displays the numbers 1 through 10 on new lines. This program uses the ++ operator to increase the variable each time the loop goes through. Notice that I created the variable before the loop began. If I had done this inside the loop, the `$counter` variable would continually be set to 1 at the beginning of each iteration of the loop.

for

The for loop is very similar to while, except that you do not need to create or increase the variable outside of the main loop statement: Everything is done inside the beginning statement of the for loop. They are optimized for counting situations in which you know exactly how many times you want to execute some code. Instead, you actually define the variable and increment it. Let's look at the for loop structure:

```
for (variable assignment; comparison test; variable change)
{
//execute statements
}
```

Doesn't look too bad, huh? Put the loop in a program. We will create an HTML form that lets the user enter any two numbers. As long as the second number is larger than the first, the PHP page will display all numbers from the first to the second number. Let's take a look at the source. The first page is for the HTML document:

```
<html>

<head>
<title>Counter of two arbitrary numbers</title>
</head>

<body>
<form name="numbers" method="get" action="phpft07-06.php">
<p>
Enter your first value:
<input type="text" name="first" />
<p>
Enter your second value:
<input type="text" name="second" />
<p>
<input type="submit" >
</form>

</body>

</html>
```

As you can see here, all we have to do is create two textboxes that contain numbers. Figure 7.9 shows what the page looks like.

The next page is the PHP code:

```
<html>
<head>
<title>Arbitrary Counter</title>
</head>

<body>
<?php

//Store variables
$a = $_GET['first'];
$b = $_GET['second'];
```

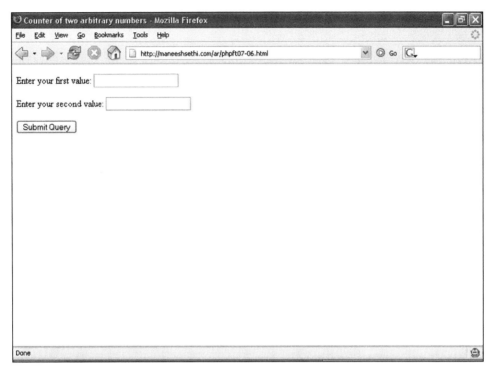

Figure 7.9
The `phpft07-06.html` file.

```
//if b is greater than a, loop through everything from a to b
if ($b > $a)
{

    for ($i = $a; $i <= $b; $i++)
    {

        echo "$i<br />";
    }
}
//b must be greater than a! Error if not.
else
{
    echo "Your second number is not greater than your first number. Please enter in
      new numbers.";

}
?>

</body>
</html>
```

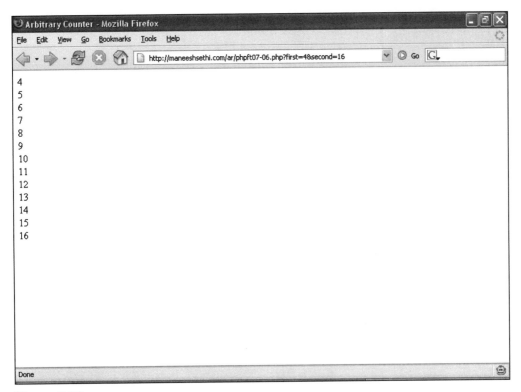

Figure 7.10
The `phpft07-06.php` file.

This page initially tests to see if the second number is larger than the first. If this is true, it creates a `for` loop that counts through all of the numbers and displays them, one after another. If this is false, it simply `echoes` out an error statement. Figure 7.10 shows what this page looks like with the first value being 4 and the second being 16.

do...while

The do...while loop is almost identical to the regular while loop except for one thing: This loop always executes at least once—even if the condition is false. Let's look at the structure:

```
do
{
//execute statements
} while (condition is true);
```

For example, if we were using `while`, what would happen if we wrote the following code?

```
$x = 10;
while($x < 10)
{
echo $x;
}
```

This will obviously do nothing, because `$x` starts off at 10. The `while` condition is never true and the `echo` statements never execute. What if we use a `do...while` loop, however?

```
$x = 10;
do
{
echo $x;
} while ($x < 10);
```

This code would simply display a counter from 1 to 10.

Note

---

foreach is a specialized type of loop that only works with arrays, so I go over it in Chapter 10.

---

break and continue

There are two rare commands that deal with loops: `break` and `continue`. You might remember `break` from the `switch` statement: When using it, the `switch` command finished and exited. The same thing happens within loops. `break` causes a loop to break out of the loop immediately. `continue`, on the other hand, immediately forces the loop to go back to the top and execute from the beginning, skipping the rest of the loop for that individual iteration.

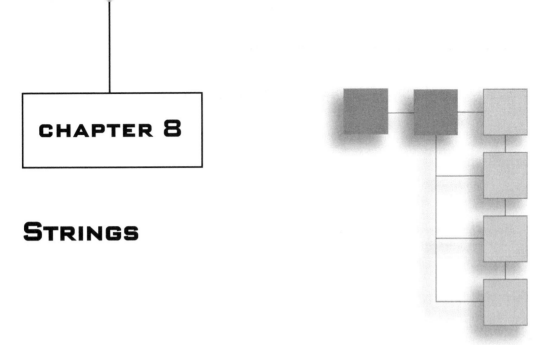

CHAPTER 8

STRINGS

Strings are a data type, much like integers or floating-point values, except they do not deal with numbers. Instead, they deal with characters and words. An example of a very basic string is a. A more complex string might be Hello, World, while a very complex string might have symbols in it that aren't even letters. They also can contain numbers. You might want to create a string that looks something like this: My house has 2 stories and 5 bedrooms.. Strings allow you to store numbers as characters inside your strings, but strings with numbers inside them are not the same as integers. Combining two strings gives you a result that is not the same as adding two numbers, so "10"+"14" does not equal 24, but 10+14 will. Be aware of the quotation marks around strings.

PHP, unlike other languages, has no length limit on strings. You can make them as long or as short as you like. This is great for when you want to turn an entire web page's source or a very long piece of text into a string.

Making Strings

There are a few methods of creating a string, and these methods are known as different methods of *syntax:*

- Single quoted

- Double quoted

- Heredoc

If you want to display a variable, you use the $ symbol. If you want to display a string, you use quotation marks. However, there are two forms of quotation marks: single and double. Both do different things, so let's go over one at a time.

Single-Quoted Syntax

Single quotation marks look like one apostrophe that appears before the string and another at the end. For example, your string might look like this:

```
'Hello, I am a string!'
```

As you can see, these single quotation marks designate the endpoints of a string. You can also create a variable that holds the string:

```
$stringvar = 'Hello, I am a string!';
```

Displaying a string is just as easy: simply use the echo function:

```
echo 'Hello, I am a string!';
```

Or, if you already created it as a variable, you can do this:

```
echo $stringvar;
```

One of the cool things you can do with single-quoted strings is embed new lines directly into the string. The new lines appear directly as you want them to.

```
echo 'Hello, I am a
string. You can see several new
lines within me. Aren't they
cool?
';
```

As you can see here, we are echoing these new lines within the middle of the string. We can set it up to deal with variables, also:

```
$stringvar = 'Hello, I am a
string. You can see several new
lines within me. Aren't they
cool?
';

echo $stringvar;
```

Pretty cool, huh? See what this looks like on the web page in Figure 8.1.

Uh oh! It removed them all and simply wrote a full statement. Why is the web page not displaying the new lines correctly? Let's check out the source in Figure 8.2 to see what it looks like.

Well, that looks better, huh? All of the new lines are there as planned, but for some reason, the web page comes out with all of the new lines gone. This occurs because an HTML browser does not deal with white space; instead, it

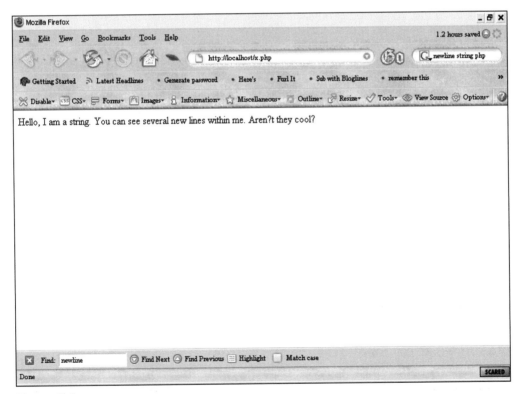

Figure 8.1
Using new lines in a string.

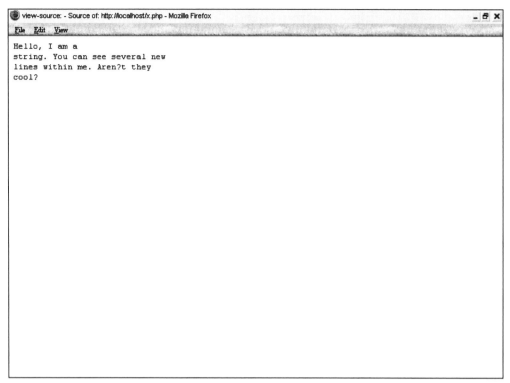

Figure 8.2
Using new lines in a string and its source.

automatically removes it all. There are a couple ways to fix this problem. The first way is to use <br /> tags and manually put them into the code. Check out how that would look:

```
$stringvar = 'Hello, I am a <br />
string. You can see several new <br />
lines within me. Aren't they <br />
cool? <br />
';

echo $stringvar;
```

Sure, this works fine, but it is a little tough to use. It's annoying to have to enter <br /> every single time you need to have a new line! Fortunately, PHP offers another way to get around this problem: a function called nl2br(). Look at the function name and see if you can figure out what it means—that's right, it converts new lines (nl) to (2)
 tags (br).

What does this mean? You can echo directly out your string and it will display the new lines as intended! For example, doing something like the following displays the text exactly how we want it:

```
echo 'Hello
I am
On
Several lines.';
```

Let's try adding this to our web page:

```
$stringvar = 'Hello, I am a
string. You can see several new
lines within me. Aren't they
cool?
';

echo nl2br($stringvar);
```

Figure 8.3 shows what this ends up looking like on the web page—working just as we wanted it to, with all the new lines showing perfectly. Let's even take a look at the source in Figure 8.4.

Not bad at all, eh? Now look closely at the document we just created. Sure, it has the new lines working fine, but there is one small error. This is one of the lines:

```
lines within me. Aren?t they
```

This is what it should be instead:

```
lines within me. Aren't they
```

Uh oh! Why did that question mark appear?

I copied and pasted the word aren't from a word processor. A lot of word processors make text look prettier by curving the apostrophes, so that instead of making a single quote straight ('), you get one that is curved ('). This is a great effect when writing documents, but in PHP, both the straight and the curved single quotes (also called *apostrophes*) are recognized as different characters. This error can occur whenever you have quotes *anywhere* in your page. Make sure you don't copy from a word processor!

In fact, the curved quote mark is not recognized as a valid character in PHP. When the PHP document gets to this quotation mark, it displays a question

Figure 8.3
Using n12br().

mark. So what would have happened if I had not used a curved quotation mark, but rather a straight one? It would have been worse. PHP would have seen this mark and assumed it was designating the end of the string. Then, it would have seen the words after the string and unsuccessfully tried to interpret them. So, instead, it would have given the following error:

Parse error: syntax error, unexpected T_STRING in **file.php** on line 5

This is obviously much worse. There must be a way to display apostrophes within a PHP document, right? Of course there is. PHP offers an escape sequence. Most escape sequences are used in double-quote syntax, but the apostrophe escape sequence is used in single-quote syntax. An *escape sequence* is a single character that tells PHP that the following character is meant to be displayed in a special way. In this case, the escape character is the backslash \. When you want to use apostrophes in your document, use \'. Let's add to what we have created. This is our final page, and you can find it on the CD as phpft08-01.php.

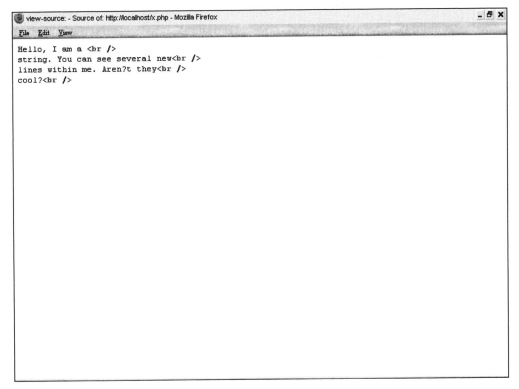

Figure 8.4
The nl2br() source.

```
<!DOCTYPE html PUBLIC "-//W3C//DTD XHTML 1.0 Strict//EN"
    "http://www.w3.org/TR/xhtml1/DTD/xhtml1-strict.dtd">
<html>
<head>
<title>Using single quote syntax</title>
</head>

<body>
<?php
$stringvar = 'Hello, I am a
string. You can see several new
lines within me. Aren\'t they
cool?
';

echo nl2br($stringvar);
?>
</body>
</html>
```

Figure 8.5
The `phpft08-01.php` file.

See that? The escape sequence makes it work better. Figure 8.5 shows what this page looks like when you load it within your web browser.

Now let's talk about using variables with single-quote syntax. As you might remember, when using single quotes, you have to be careful about putting variables into strings. Instead of simply putting the variable in, you need to join it to the rest of the string using the dot operator (.). This is a little tricky, so pay attention.

Begin a string with a single quote and end it with a single quote. You then use the dot operator to join the two. For example, I want to put a variable `$name` into a document. I basically want the page to say "Welcome to www.maneeshsethi.com , `$name`" where `$name` is replaced with the user's name. See how the dots join the variable—which is not within quotes—to the strings—which are within quotes?

```
echo 'Welcome to maneeshsethi.com, ' . $name . '!';
```

Okay, let's make an example program that does exactly this. We will have a page into which you enter your name, and the next page welcomes you by the name you entered. Let's take a look at the form first. This page is phpft08-02.html on the CD. See Figure 8.6.

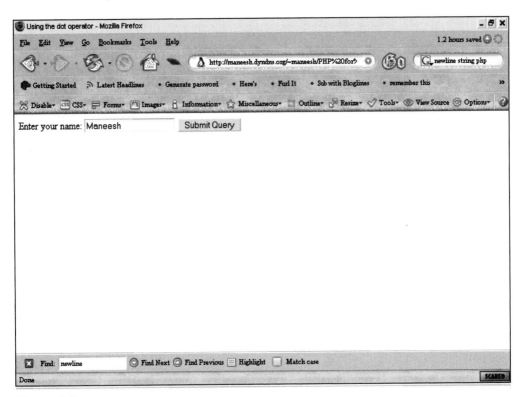

Figure 8.6
The phpft08-02.html file.

```
<!DOCTYPE html PUBLIC "-//W3C//DTD XHTML 1.0 Strict//EN"
    "http://www.w3.org/TR/xhtml1/DTD/xhtml1-strict.dtd">
<html>
<head>
<title>Using the dot operator</title>
</head>


<body>
<form name="nameofuser" action="phpft08-02.php" method="get">
    Enter your name: <input type="text" name="username">
    <input type="submit">
</form>
</body>
</html>
```

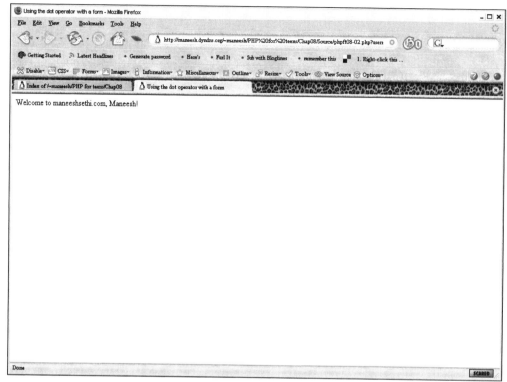

Figure 8.7
The `phpft08-02.php` file.

We just created a form with an input value. Let's add the PHP document to that, `phpft08-02.php`, then check out how it looks in Figure 8.7:

```
<!DOCTYPE html PUBLIC "-//W3C//DTD XHTML 1.0 Strict//EN"
    "http://www.w3.org/TR/xhtml1/DTD/xhtml1-strict.dtd">
<html>
<head>
<title>Using the dot operator with a form</title>
</head>

<body>
<?php

$name = $_GET['username'];

echo 'Welcome to maneeshsethi.com, ' . $name . '!';
```

```
?>
</body>
</html>
```

Double-Quoted Syntax

Double-quoted syntax has these differences from single-quote syntax:

- Many more escape sequences.

- The way that variables are parsed. Parsing means displaying variables, and double quotes deal with the variables in a different (and easier) fashion.

- A different way of dealing with variables. Table 8.1 lists the escape sequences available when using double-quote syntax. Try to memorize those you will use.

Table 8.1 Common Escape Sequences

Sequence	Name
\n	Line feed
\r	Carriage return
\t	Horizontal tab
\\	Backslash
\$	Dollar sign
\"	Double quote

Note

There are two other double-quote syntax escape sequences, but they deal with numbers of a different base.

You can use variable names directly in a string simply by referring to them with a $ symbol. If I want to refer to the variable $name within a program, this is what I could do:

```
echo "My name is $name";
```

Pretty cool, huh? You don't need to worry at all about using the dot operator, nor using any special symbols for your variable. You can do a few cool things with double-quoted syntax. For example, take a look at the following script:

```
$stringvar = car;

echo "I want to buy six $stringvars";
```

This doesn't work as we want. We want the result to say "I want to buy six cars", but instead we get an error. PHP has a way to fix this:

```
$stringvar = car;

echo "I want to buy six ${stringvar}s;
```

The trick here is to use curly braces: { and }. By using them, you can display the variables as you want. Another way to do this is to use concatenation like we did with the single-quote syntax. The previous example could be done like this:

```
$stringvar = car;

echo "I want to buy six $stringvar" . "s";
```

As you can see, we bypass this problem altogether by using the dot operator!

String Functions

A lot of functions can enhance a string's capabilities. One very common need is to convert an integer into a string. This may happen when you take in an integer from a form and need to add it to part of a string. Fortunately, there is a function that can do this: strval(). Let's put this in a quick program. Watch what happens if we have the user enter two numbers. The program adds them together and combines the results of strval(). The first page is a simple HTML page. The following code creates a page that looks like Figure 8.8:

```
<!DOCTYPE html PUBLIC "-//W3C//DTD XHTML 1.0 Strict//EN"
    "http://www.w3.org/TR/xhtml1/DTD/xhtml1-strict.dtd">
<html>

<head>
<title>Putting two numbers together with strval()</title>
</head>

<body>

<form name="together" action="phpft08-03.php" method="get">

        Enter your first number: <input type="text" name="firstop">
        <p>Enter your second number: <input type="text" name="secondop">
        <p><input type="submit">
```

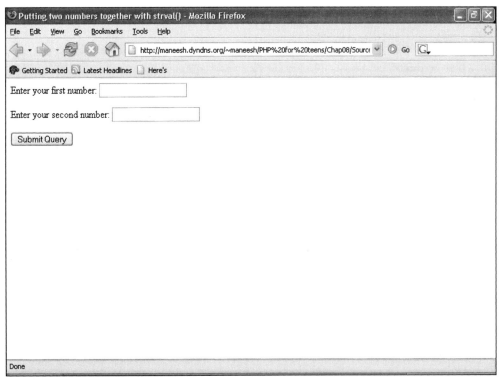

Figure 8.8
The `phpft08-03.html` file.

```
</form>
</body>

</html>
```

Now, let's take a look at the PHP document:

```
<html>
<head>
<title>Using strval()</title>
</head>
<body>
<?php

$a = $_GET['firstop'];
$b = $_GET['secondop'];

echo "Let's take a look at the two results of using your operators.";
echo "<p>Using the addition operator does this: ".( $a + $b);
```

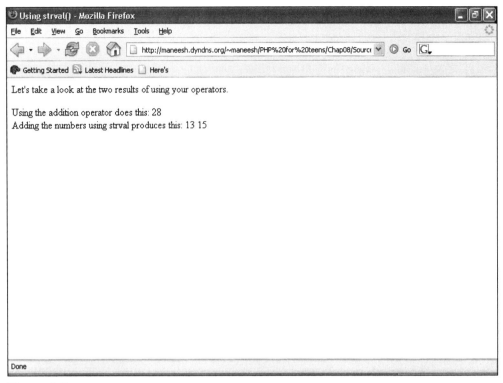

Figure 8.9
The `phpft08-03.php` file.

```
echo "<br>Adding the numbers using strval produces this: ". strval($a).' '.
strval($b);
?>
</body>

</html>
```

This page, with the inputs of 13 and 15, looks like Figure 8.9.

You see what this program does? In the echoing section, adding two numbers creates an addition problem. However, using their strval() values, you get a new sentence!

This is only one of the possible string functions, and there are several dozen more. Some are really cool, such as substr(), which lets you search within a string, and soundex(), which lets you find words that have similar pronunciations. I recommend researching www.maneeshsethi.com and www.php.net to learn some more useful techniques for strings.

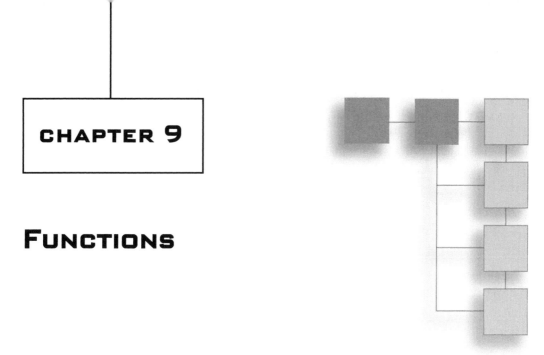

CHAPTER 9

FUNCTIONS

A *function* is essentially a section of code that you can call over and over again. This function can do repetitive tasks very easily and safely, and because it is encapsulated in a function name, it makes the main program look a lot neater.

We have been using a lot of predefined functions, written by PHP, such as `strval()` and `nl2br()`. Notice how both functions have parentheses after the name? That is a function's defining attribute. In Chapter 6 I explain that I format my multi-word functions using an underscore. This is an example of one of my functions:

```
execute_func();
```

Designing Your Own Functions

You might be wondering why you would ever want to design a function. Functions allow your program to become a lot more robust and capable. Functions make your program *modular,* meaning that you can use parts of your program in other programs without worrying about problems. This means less work for you overall. Let's take an example. Let's say I had a program that added the numbers 1 through 10. This is how a sample program would look if I wrote it without functions:

```
<?php
echo "The following counter will add up the numbers 1 through 10";
echo "<br>Please wait, your numbers are being tabulated below.";
```

```
$runningcounter=0;
for ( $x=1; $x <= 10; $x++)
{
    $runningcounter = $runningcounter + $x;
}
echo '<p>Your result is ' . $runningcounter;
echo "<br>Thanks for using our program!";
?>
```

The majority of this program is taken up by the code for the running counter. The counter also does not seem to mix well with the rest of the program that consists solely of echo statements. The program would look like the one in Figure 9.1.

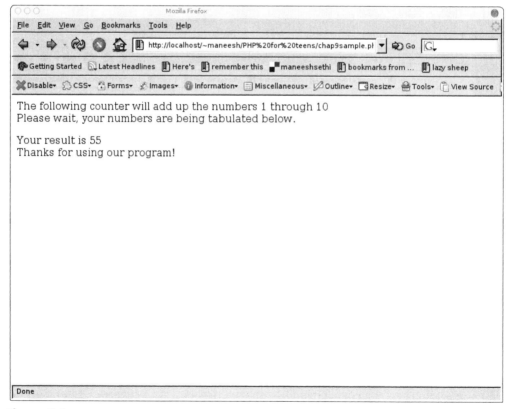

Figure 9.1
A running counter program without using a function in phpft09-01.php.

As you can see, the display looks fine. Underneath, as you saw before, the code isn't as nice as it could be. Look at how we could make this program look a heck of a lot better by turning the counter into a function:

```php
<?php
echo "The following counter will add up the numbers 1 through 10";
echo "<br>Please wait, your numbers are being tabulated below.";
echo '<p>Your result is ' . counter_1_10();
echo "<br>Thanks for using our program!";
?>
```

This might look a little strange. The only change is removing the code for the `for` loop from the earlier program and replacing it with a function call. The call is in the `echo` statement.

```php
echo '<p>Your result is ' . counter_1_10();
```

You can see here we changed the variable $x to counter_1_10(). Of course, this function name by itself doesn't do anything—we need to make it actually mean something! I show you, very soon, how to make your functions work, but before I do, look at another example of using functions.

If you are writing a song, you could do something like this:

```php
<?php
verse1();
chorus();
verse2();
chorus();
verse3();
chorus();
chorus();
?>
```

This is a pretty common setup for a song, but notice how you are allowed to call the same function chorus() multiple times, and in any order? Functions allow you to do cool things like this.

Before you learn how to create this program, look at the basic structure for defining a function. The parts you can change to suit your individual function are in italics.

```
<?php
function function_name(parameter1,parameter2,...)
{
function code
}
?>
```

Doesn't seem too difficult, does it? Function definitions are just the structure and code of the function.

Dissecting a Function

Functions have three parts that we need to go over:

- Function code

- Parameter list

- Return value

Only the code section is required; both the parameter list and the return value are optional. However, in most functions, you will be using all three.

Function Code

The function code section is the main section located between the curly braces: { and }. This section deals with the function's actual work. You can add statements and expressions in this section as you would in a normal section of the code. Often, this section of the code interacts with the parameter list in the function declaration.

Parameter List

Parameters are variables and values that you can pass to a function when calling it. Remember when we used the nl2br() function? This function converted new lines in your code to <br> tags, taking the string that had new lines in it as a parameter. You pass parameters inside the parentheses when you call the function, and the function can then use the parameters to act upon it.

In using the nl2br() function, you might create a string and send it to the function like this:

```php
<?php
$stringvar = 'Hello
I am a string
that has new lines inside
of it';

echo nl2br($stringvar);
?>
```

In this example, the variable $stringvar acts as a parameter and is passed to the nl2br() function. However, notice that the *result* is echoed by the echo construct. You create a result from a function by using a return value. Many functions use a return value if they produce a result.

Return Value

Return values are the opposite of parameters. When you use a parameter, you are sending data to the function to be acted upon. A *return value* is data sent from the function to the program that called it. The program uses the result to go on with its actions. In the case of nl2br(), the return value was the new string. In the case of the program we wrote, the return value is as follows:

```
'Hello <br />
I am a string <br />
that has new lines inside <br />
of it';
```

This result is then echoed out by the echo statement. This causes the display in Figure 9.2. Because of the function's return value, the echo statement is able to do its job and display the proper code.

Let's take a look at the web page we created earlier in this chapter. In that program, we created a running counter to display the value of the sum of all numbers between 1 and 10. By removing the counter and replacing it with a variable, we made the program a lot easier on the eyes: The coding section was exported into a function, and the main section was executed with a function call. We still need to declare and display that function on the screen, however. Take a look at how the full program looks with the main section's code and the function's code in place:

```php
<?php
echo "The following counter will add up the numbers 1 through 10";
echo "<br>Please wait, your numbers are being tabulated below.";
```

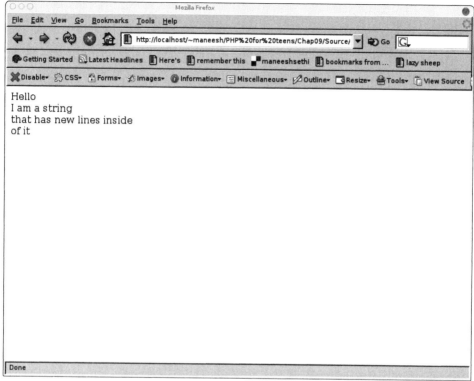

Figure 9.2
Using a return value in a function.

```
echo '<p>Your result is ' . counter_1_10();
echo "<br>Thanks for using our program!";

function counter_1_10()
{
    $runningcounter=0;
    for ( $x=1; $x <= 10; $x++)
    {
        $runningcounter = $runningcounter + $x;
    }

return $runningcounter;
}
?>
```

The program has expanded a little bit, huh? Well, it has, but the expansion has caused it to be a lot cleaner. The new function takes care of all the code and you can concentrate only on the main program to see what is going on.

The function here is defined as `counter_1_10()` and it does the same thing as the running counter we developed earlier. The only difference is that it also uses a return value near the end of the script. The following line makes the return magic happen:

```
return $runningcounter;
```

The variable `$runningcounter` contains the sum that we have been looking for throughout the function. We return the value back to where it was called up in the `echo` statement in the main program. The value of the returned data (in this case, 55) is substituted for the function call, and the `echo` statement echoes out the correct result. The web page looks like the one in Figure 9.3.

Hey, that looks a lot like Figure 9.1! Actually, they are identical. If you are writing code and you get the feeling that you should copy and paste some code from earlier in your script, that is a perfect time to use a function! A function just

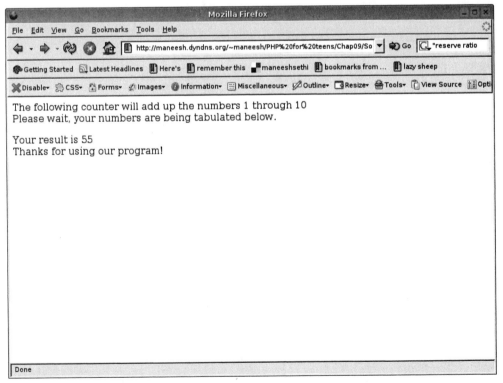

Figure 9.3
Using a return value in `phpft09-03.php`.

splits up the section where the code occurs to make the program make more sense.

This may seem pointless. Why split it up if all it does is make the program a little longer? Well, for one, the program is cleaner when using functions. However, the real power in using functions comes when you combine return values with parameters and make the functions more flexible.

Let's rewrite this program to deal with an HTML page, allowing input from the user. The user can enter a lower value and an upper value, and the program will add all numbers between the two and show the result. Let's start off by looking at the HTML page, shown in Figure 9.4. It's similar to ones we have seen in the past.

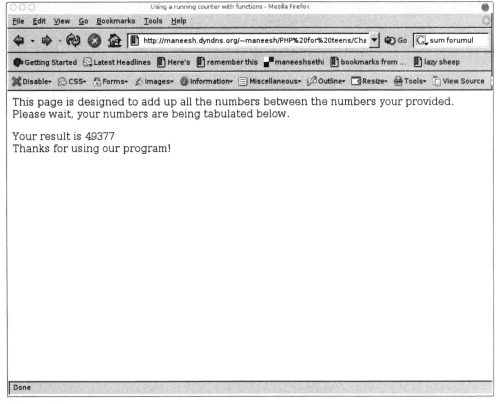

Figure 9.4
Designing the form in `phpft09-03.html`.

```
<!DOCTYPE html PUBLIC "-//W3C//DTD XHTML 1.0 Strict//EN"
    "http://www.w3.org/TR/xhtml1/DTD/xhtml1-strict.dtd">
<html>

<head>
<title>Using parameters on a running number counter</title>
</head>

<body>

<form name="together" action="phpft09-03.php" method="get">

    Enter your first number: <input type="text" name="firstop">
    <p>Enter your second number: <input type="text" name="secondop">
    <p><input type="submit">

</form>
</body>

</html>
```

Now display the result of the two numbers in the following PHP document:

```
<!DOCTYPE html PUBLIC "-//W3C//DTD XHTML 1.0 Strict//EN"
    "http://www.w3.org/TR/xhtml1/DTD/xhtml1-strict.dtd">
<html>
<head>
<title>Using a running counter with functions</title>
</head>

<body>

This page is designed to add up all the numbers between the numbers you provided.
<br>Please wait, your numbers are being tabulated below.

<?php

    $first = $_GET['firstop'];
    $second = $_GET['secondop'];

    if ($second > $first) //if the second number is larger than the first, execute
      the program as it should run
    {
```

```
    echo '<p>Your result is ' . running_counter($first,$second);
    echo "<br>Thanks for using our program!";

    }

    else //the second number is not larger than the first, error

    {

    echo "<p><font color=\"red\"> Your second number is not larger than the first
      number, please fix and try again.</font>";

    }


    function running_counter($first,$second)
    {
        $runningcounter=0;
        for ( $x=$first; $x <= $second; $x++)
        {
            $runningcounter = $runningcounter + $x;
        }

    return $runningcounter;

    }

?>


</body>
</html>
```

Pretty tricky, huh? This has been our most complex program so far, and it is one of the coolest. This function lets you find the sum of any two arbitrary numbers using a simple for loop. Check out Figure 9.5. The figure shows the result using the numbers 13 and 314. The result, as shown, is the sum of every number between 13 and 314. Doing this by hand would take forever!

The program has a basic body, utilizing the main section only to access the variables and echo results. The function it calls takes in two parameters, $first and $second, and uses these parameters to return a sum. This function could be used in any program that needs the sum of all digits between two numbers.

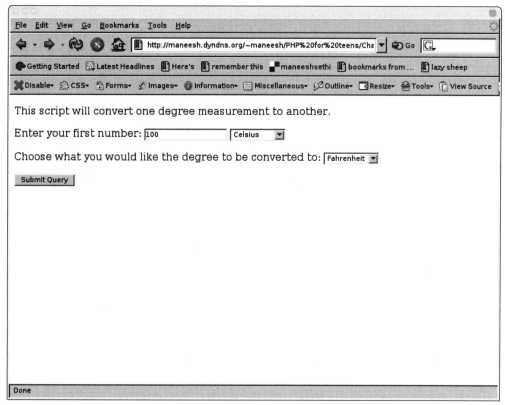

Figure 9.5
The sum in `phpft09-03.php`.

Notice that we called the function with variables $first and $second, and the function used variables of the same name. This is not required. We can pass whatever parameters we want into the function, and the values that we pass are copied into the variable names of the function declaration. We could have chosen simply to pass $_GET['firstop'] and $_GET['secondop'] rather than ever turning them into the scalar variables $first and $second, for example. We converted the $_GET variables because they are a lot easier to handle without the bracketed array syntax and because their names are more intuitive.

The real strength of using functions comes from their portability. Because a function can be written so that it does not rely on any variables from the program, you can simply lift that function right out of this script and use it on another. If you ever write another program that requires a counter, you can use this same function *without modification*. In fact, a lot of programmers take all of their commonly used functions and build a library file with them. Then, whenever they need to perform a task, they simply load up the library file and call the already written function.

Of course, not all functions are portable because of something called *variable scope*. When using variables, the program can only access a subset of the variables that are created. For example, if you have a variable $test_var in function DoA(), another function DoB() cannot access that $test_var unless the variable is passed as a parameter to DoB(). Some arrays that are predefined by the language, such as $_GET and $_POST, are global to all functions. However, for functions you develop on your own, be careful to make sure you only access and use variables in scope.

For the mathematically minded

If you look at the program we created, you can see it's a pretty ugly way to get a sum of all the numbers between arbitrary endpoints. We use a mechanism that actually loops through each value and adds it to a running counter. A few mathematical functions will produce the correct result without the ugly loops. This means that for very large sums, this program could take a while.

To get the sum from this series, there is a cool mathematical formula: sum. This is how it appears: S(n) = n/2 * (a(1) + a(n)), where n is the total of numbers you want to add together, a(1) is the first number in the series, and a(n) is the final number in the series. If you want to find the sum of the first four members of the series we wrote, you would get this: S(4) = 4/2 * (1 + 7) = 16. If you use this formula in your running calculation, the answer will be achieved much more quickly.

So what's the point? Just because a solution works doesn't mean it is the fastest or best way to do something. Sometimes things can go much faster if you find a better algorithm.

Calling a Function Depending on a Condition

Sometimes you need to call a function depending on a condition. You'll often need to write more than one function in a program. We don't need to call all of them in every run, but we may need to call a few depending on the situation.

One of the best examples is when you need to convert Celsius to Fahrenheit or vice versa: a degree-conversion calculator. The first thing to do is design the HTML page. This is going to be complex because it gives the user lots of options to convert. Let's take a look at the HTML file it takes to produce this. You can find this on the CD as phpft09-04.html.

```
<!DOCTYPE html PUBLIC "-//W3C//DTD XHTML 1.0 Strict//EN"
    "http://www.w3.org/TR/xhtml1/DTD/xhtml1-strict.dtd">
```

```
<html>

<head>
<title>A Degree Calculator</title>
</head>

<body>

<form name="together" action="phpft09-04.php" method="get">
      <p>This script will convert one degree measurement to another.
      <p>Enter your first number: <input type="text" name="firstdeg">

      <select name="firsttype">
      <option value="celsius">Celsius
      <option value="fahrenheit">Fahrenheit

      </select>

      <p>Choose what you would like the degree to be converted to:

      <select name="secondtype">
      <option value="celsius">Celsius
      <option value="fahrenheit">Fahrenheit
      </select>


      <p><input type="submit">

</form>
</body>
</html>
```

This page looks like Figure 9.6.

You might be wondering why we allow the user to choose what he converts the degree measurement to. Why not automatically choose to convert to Fahrenheit if she selects Fahrenheit? This allows for expandability. If you want to let the user convert to a different degree measurement, such as Kelvin, you can easily add this without changing the HTML page very much.

The PHP for this page is very complex and involves a lot of functions. Let's go through the major parts one at a time. The first section involves setting up the HTML and synchronizing the variables.

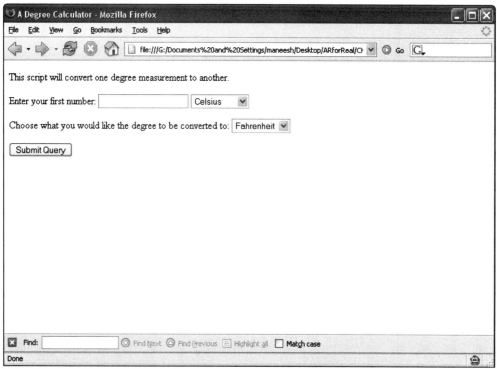

Figure 9.6
Conversion form in `phpft09-04.html`.

```
<!DOCTYPE html PUBLIC "-//W3C//DTD XHTML 1.0 Strict//EN"
    "http://www.w3.org/TR/xhtml1/DTD/xhtml1-strict.dtd">
<html>
<head>
<title>Conversions of degrees</title>
</head>

<body>

We are going to convert your value as you requested. Please wait.<p>

<?php

$a = $_GET['firstdeg'];
$firstdeg = $_GET['firsttype'];
$seconddeg = $_GET['secondtype'];
```

This section creates the page and sets up some basic variables for the remainder of the program. We use the $_GET[] array to take in the user's input from the previous page. Next, we need to deal with these variables.

```
//DECLARE CONDITIONS
if ($firstdeg == 'celsius' && $seconddeg == 'fahrenheit')
{
        echo "The conversion of $a degrees $firstdeg to $seconddeg is " .
celsius_to_fahrenheit($a) . ".";
}

else if ($firstdeg == 'fahrenheit' && $seconddeg == 'celsius')

{
        echo "The conversion of $a degrees $firstdeg to $seconddeg is " .
fahrenheit_to_celsius($a) . ".";
}

else //if they are both the same

{
        echo "Error, you are converting a degree to the same measurement.
Please change one and try again. ";

}
```

This part of the program handles the echoing out of the results of the function calls. In addition, it actually goes about interpolating the function calls between the echoed strings. Look carefully at the strings to see how the quotation marks and function calls work to make the string become a valid sentence.

The final section of the program is a listing of the functions that do the program's work:

```
function celsius_to_fahrenheit($a)
{

        return ((9/5)*$a + 32);

}

function fahrenheit_to_celsius($a)
{
```

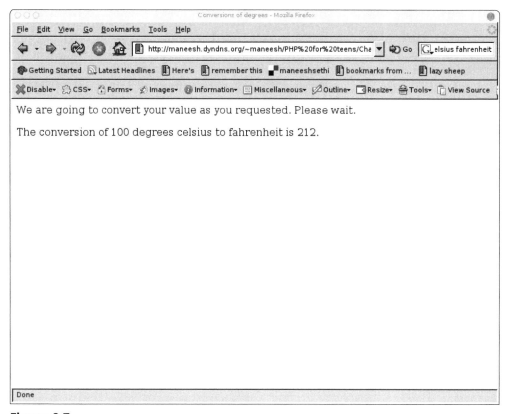

Figure 9.7
Conversion in `phpft09-04.php`.

```
        return (5.0/9.0)*($a-32);
}

?>

</body>
</html>
```

Pretty simple, huh? Check out Figure 9.7 to see what this page looks like. These two functions return the values requested by the echo calls. Their return values come from the Celsius and Fahrenheit conversion formulas, easily found in any science textbook. Together, all the parts of this PHP program create a very cool result, a form that can accept user input and deal with whatever numbers it gets. All in all, it's not bad for just a short time of learning, huh?

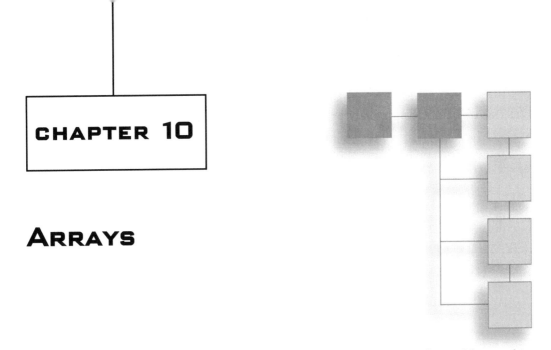

CHAPTER 10

ARRAYS

You already learned a little about arrays, those pesky little sets of variables, and in this chapter, we are going to review what we already know and learn a lot more about them. Arrays are very useful in PHP programming, and you will find them in probably every advanced program you see. When using a form to submit a value, the variables are stored in an array, which is passed along to the new page. This array is used for calculations and data recall.

PHP documentation explains an *array* as an ordered map that has a set of keys that each has a value. You create the keys in the array; *keys* are names that reference the individual items in an array. Sometimes a set of consecutive numbers is used, and other times a set of strings is used. Because all elements of an array have the same name, you need some way to keep them separate. For example, when using the `$_GET[]` array, the key was whatever was in the brackets. For example, the `$_GET['fullname']` key was `fullname`. Often, the key is a number, so you can have a set of arrays from 0 to 10 looking like `$array[0]` to `$array[10]`.

Arrays are particularly strong if you use integers with them and want to initialize a large number of values. `for` loops can do this very easily, using a `for` loop to set each individual element of an array. Arrays and loops are natural companions.

Creating an Array

To create an array, you need several elements.

`array()` Language Construct

Use the `array()` *language construct*, which is very similar to a function. You call `array()` and the return value is equal to the new array. Therefore, whatever variable you set as equal to the result of `array()` *becomes* an array. For example, take a look at the following:

```
$newarray = array();
```

Your new array will be stored in the variable `$newarray`. Of course, the problem we have now is that this array is blank! We have to create items in the array. Before we do this, let me show you how to reference items in an array.

Reference Items

Array items have two parts: a key and a value. A *key* is basically the location of the variable, and the *value* is what is stored at that location. Think of a golf course. In this case, the hole you are on is the key (1–18), and your score on the hole is the value. You can then look for a specific hole and see what your score was. Similarly, if you make a reference to a variable in your array with a valid key, a value at that location is returned. The key in this type of problem is stored within brackets attached to the end of the variable's name. Here is a simple structure:

```
$newarray['key'] = value;
```

If you substitute your wanted values, you create an array element.

Let's look at a simple program, whose results are shown in Figure 10.1. This is `phpft10-01.php`. This program simply creates five array values and echoes them on the screen.

```
<?php

$newarray = array();

$newarray[1] = "First item";
$newarray[2] = "Second item";
$newarray[3] = "Third item";
$newarray[4] = "Fourth item";
$newarray[5] = "Fifth item";

echo $newarray[1];
echo $newarray[2];
echo $newarray[3];
```

```
echo $newarray[4];
echo $newarray[5];

?>
```

That's not too difficult, huh? Creating an array just requires you to reference it using the proper syntax and set the items equal to their values.

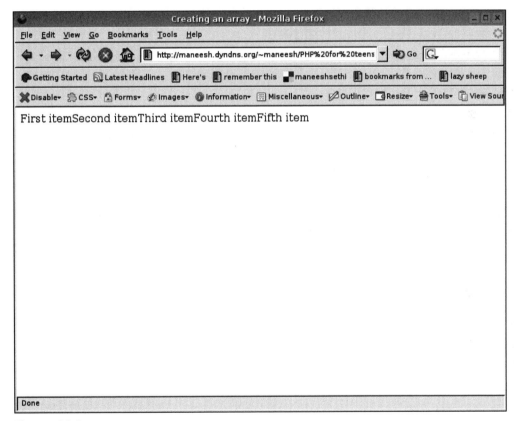

Figure 10.1
Creating array elements in `phpft10-01.php`.

Creating Array Elements

Now, in a case like earlier, you already knew what all the variables were going to equal. PHP offers a great way to create your array elements at the same time as creating arrays. This requires the => operator, and the array declaration is done at the time array() is called. Look at the basic structure:

```
$newarray = array(key => value, key => value, . . .)
```

As you can see, we are calling `array()` with a list of parameters. You can create as many keys as you want, and all of them will be part of `$newarray`.

Let's rewrite the program using this new syntax. This is `phpft10-02.php` and you can find it on the CD. In addition to changing the preceding program's syntax, I added `<br />` tags to make it cleaner.

```php
<?php

$newarray = array(1 => "First item", 2 => "Second item", 3 => "Third item", 4
  => "Fourth item", 5 => "Fifth item" );

echo $newarray[1] . '<br /> ';
echo $newarray[2] . '<br /> ';
echo $newarray[3] . '<br /> ';
echo $newarray[4] . '<br /> ';
echo $newarray[5] . '<br /> ';

?>
```

The results are shown in Figure 10.2. Pretty cool, huh? A lot less work if you already know the variable names.

Defining Arrays with PHP

I'm going to show you a couple cool tricks you can use for defining arrays like this.

Notice that this type of array uses a consecutive list of integers. When using strings or nonconsecutive integers, these tricks won't work, but when using similar lists these tricks are great.

Skip the Array Key Definition

The first trick is to skip defining the array key. When you begin defining the array with the short syntax and skip the "*key*" => part (using only a list of values), you get an array with integer indices starting at 0. For example, say you did this:

```php
$testarray = array('a','b','c','d','e');
```

You get an array with these elements:

```php
$testarray[0]='a';
$testarray[1]='b';
```

```
$testarray[2]='c';
$testarray[3]='d';
$testarray[4]='e';
```

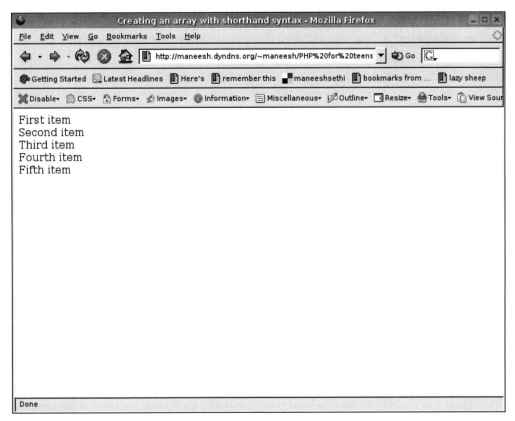

Figure 10.2
Creating array elements in `phpft10-01.php`.

The declarations are identical. Note that because we start counting with 0, a five-element array ends at array key 4.

If you want to do this without using short syntax, there is a method for that also:

```
$testarray = array();
$testarray[]='a';
$testarray[]='b';
$testarray[]='c';
$testarray[]='d';
$testarray[]='e';
```

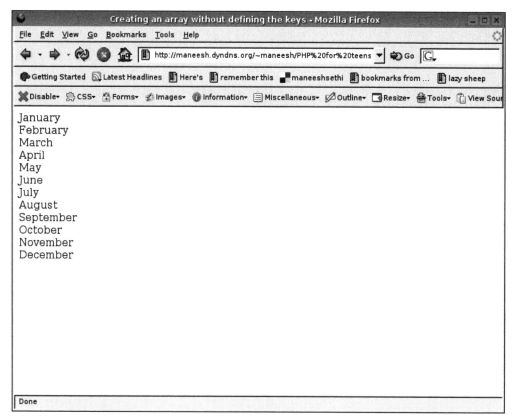

Figure 10.3
Creating array elements without keys in `phpft10-03.php`.

In this case, we just leave the key absolutely blank, and it assigns the next integer value to the array. Let's take a look at an example. The following is code from `phpft10-03.php` and it appears onscreen like Figure 10.3.

```php
<?php

$newarray = array("January", "February", "March", "April", "May", "June",
  "July"
, "August", "September", "October" , "November", "December");

echo $newarray[0] . '<br /> ';
echo $newarray[1] . '<br /> ';
echo $newarray[2] . '<br /> ';
echo $newarray[3] . '<br /> ';
echo $newarray[4] . '<br /> ';
echo $newarray[5] . '<br /> ';
echo $newarray[6] . '<br /> ';
```

```
echo $newarray[7] . '<br /> ';
echo $newarray[8] . '<br /> ';
echo $newarray[9] . '<br /> ';
echo $newarray[10] . '<br /> ';
echo $newarray[11] . '<br /> ';
?>
```

Note that in this case, the months started with 0 and ended with 12. Many times in programs it is easier to think of calendar months as 1–12, rather than 0–11. If you do this, you should probably create a blank month at month 0 and start January off at array element 1.

Numeric indices for your array are really useful when you are going to loop through all of the data and manipulate them. For example, in the golf example at the beginning of the chapter, we stored the hole number as the key and the score on that hole as a value. If we loop through all the holes from 1–18, we would get the final full score! String indices are better for describing what is stored in the array, such as with $_GET[] arrays. You have string describers, so it is easier to see what is stored in each element.

Use a Loop

Now there is one more trick involved with basic array creation and display. Notice how hard it is to type out all those echo statements? Wouldn't it be easier if you could loop through the array and display them all?

There is a special type of loop that does this, but it is more powerful and we will be going over it later on in this chapter. For now, let's use a basic for loop to make this program a lot easier to write. The following code is from phpft10-04. Check out Figure 10.4, which shows what this array looks like on the screen.

```
<?php
$newarray = array("January", "February", "March", "April", "May", "June",
  "July"
, "August", "September", "October" , "November", "December");

for ($i = 0; $i <= 11; $i++)
{
      echo $newarray[$i] . '<br /> ';
}

?>
```

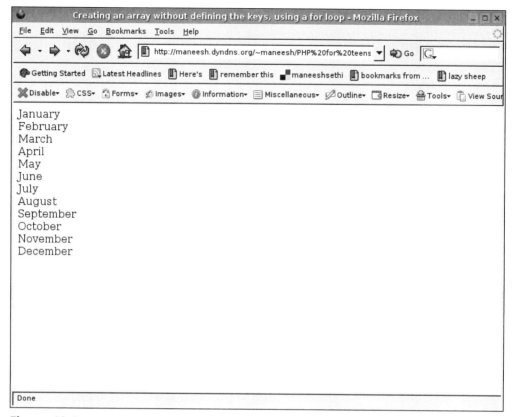

Figure 10.4
Creating array elements with a for loop phpft10-04.php.

See how this program works? A for loop goes through all the indices and elements of an array, and displays them on the screen. It's a lot easier than actually writing out each element manually.

Working with Arrays

The following functions let you use arrays in various ways throughout your program.

unset() Function

When you are done working with array values, sometimes it is nice to get rid of them altogether. You might need to use them again later in the program, and want to reuse the keys without worrying about overwriting data. PHP offers the

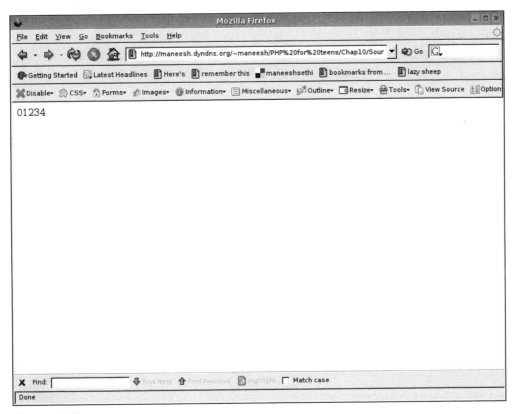

Figure 10.5
Before using unset().

unset() function to get rid of old array values (or, for that matter, old arrays). The function unset() works by only unsetting exactly the parameter you pass to it. Unsetting an array is useful for memory management.

If you want to create an array with five values, you could write something like the following, which ends up looking like Figure 10.5:

```php
<?php

$newarray[]=0;
$newarray[]=1;
$newarray[]=2;
$newarray[]=3;
$newarray[]=4;

echo $newarray[0];
echo $newarray[1];
```

```
echo $newarray[2];
echo $newarray[3];
echo $newarray[4];

?>
```

Now, let's use unset() on this program:

```
<?php

$newarray[]=0;
$newarray[]=1;
$newarray[]=2;
$newarray[]=3;
$newarray[]=4;

unset($newarray[2]);
unset($newarray[3]);

echo $newarray[0];
echo $newarray[1];
echo $newarray[2];
echo $newarray[3];
echo $newarray[4];

?>
```

All we did here was add a couple of lines on unsetting some array items. The result is in Figure 10.6.

If this program gives you an error, that means that your server has its restrictions set very high. This error arises when you try to echo out unset variables. However, this means it is working correctly—an error should occur if your server has strict settings.

This page can be found in phpft10-05.php on the CD. As you see, simply the act of unsetting the variables made trying to echo them impossible, because they did not exist. You could've gone one step further, however, and eliminated the entire array by doing this:

```
unset($newarray);
```

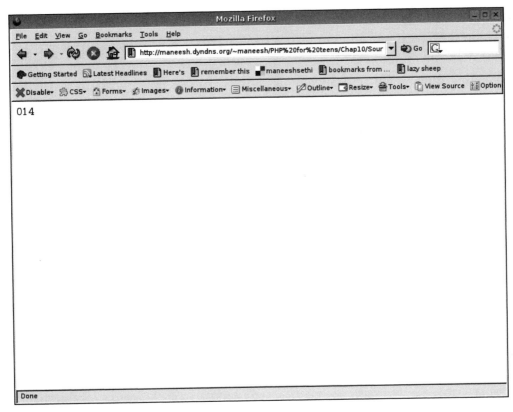

Figure 10.6
After using `unset()` in `phpft10-05.php`.

foreach Loop

The foreach loop is designed distinctly for working with arrays, and if you know how to use it, you can do many more things with arrays. foreach lets you choose any array that you have designed and independently loop through every single item in the array. This is great if you have developed an array of an unknown amount of items and simply want to display the array's contents as soon as possible.

The foreach loop has two separate structures, both of which you can use at any time. The first structure looks like this:

```
foreach ($arrayname as $valuename)
{
        //perform statements
}
```

Take a look at that! I just created a new loop that goes through every single one of the loop's elements and allows me to access each one. The value $arrayname is the name of the array, and $valuename is an arbitrary variable that is assigned to each individual value of the loop in each iteration.

Let's see how we might use this. Let's go back to the web page we made earlier, phpft10-03.php. In this script, we developed a page that would display each month of the year. We used a dozen echo commands to display each one. However, using the foreach loop, we could do this much quicker—more quickly, in fact, than a basic for loop like the one we developed in phpft10-04.php. Check out Figure 10.7 and look at the code that would do this. This page is phpft10-05.php on the CD.

```
<!DOCTYPE html PUBLIC "-//W3C//DTD XHTML 1.0 Strict//EN"
    "http://www.w3.org/TR/xhtml1/DTD/xhtml1-strict.dtd">

<html>
<head>
<title>Using a foreach loop</title>
</head>

<body>

<?php


$newarray = array("January", "February", "March", "April", "May", "June",
"July", "August", "September", "October" , "November", "December");


$variablecounter = 1;
foreach ($newarray as $month)
{
echo "We have iterated through the loop $variablecounter times ==> ";
echo $month . '<br />';
$variablecounter++;
}

?>


</body>
</html>
```

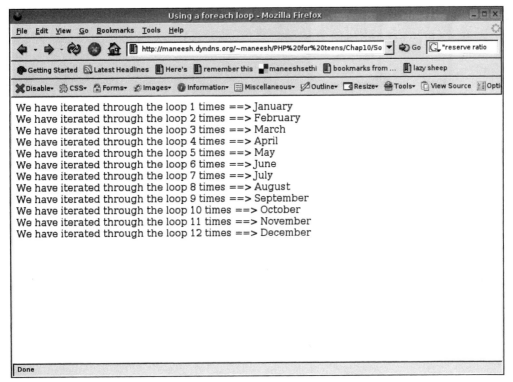

Figure 10.7
Using the foreach loop in phpft10-05.php.

Hey, pretty cool, huh? We developed the same item and used a variable counter to actually count the number of times we looped through. The counter increments itself each time the loop is iterated, so we see the number of times that every command occurs. This is a lot easier than using the basic for loop, huh? Let's take a look at the other possible structure you can use for defining foreach loops in your programs:

```
foreach ($arrayname as $keyname ==> $valuename)
{
        //perform statements
}
```

A little different declaration. The only major difference here is that we added $keyname; now we can figure out the keys as well as the values. This structure is great for using with forms.

Let's see a sample. We could develop a form that has several optional items. It can then display the keys and values to help understand which fields were filled in and which the user decided to leave blank. Create a sample form. The following code comes from phpft10-06.html:

```
<!DOCTYPE html PUBLIC "-//W3C//DTD XHTML 1.0 Strict//EN"
    "http://www.w3.org/TR/xhtml1/DTD/xhtml1-strict.dtd">

<html>
<head>
<title>Using a form with foreach</title>
</head>

<body>
<form name="sampleform" action="phpft10-06.php" method="get">

<h2>Please enter in the following information. All fields are optional. </h2>
Name: <input type="text" name="name">
<br>Address: <input type="text" name="address">
<p>Phone number:
<br><input type="text" name="phone">
<br>I prefer a) <input type="radio" name="prefer" value="cheese">Cheese
<br>b) <input type="radio" name="prefer" value="bread">Bread
<br>c) <input type="radio" name="prefer" value="meat">Meat
<input type="submit">
</form>

</body>
</html>
```

This page creates a nice-looking form with radio buttons. Check out what this page looks like in Figure 10.8.

Let's look at the PHP section of phpft10-06.php, which displays the results using PHP:

```
<!DOCTYPE html PUBLIC "-//W3C//DTD XHTML 1.0 Strict//EN"
    "http://www.w3.org/TR/xhtml1/DTD/xhtml1-strict.dtd">

<html>
<head>
<title>Using a foreach loop with forms</title>
</head>

<body>
```

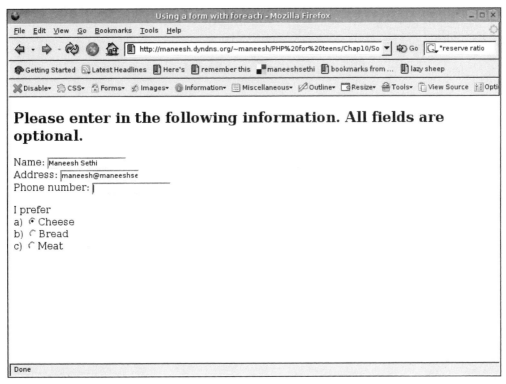

Figure 10.8
Creating a form for `phpft10-06.html`.

```php
<?php

$counter = 1;
foreach($_GET as $keyvalue => $realvalue)
{

      echo "Loop has iterated $counter times: ";
      echo "Key: $keyvalue has value: $realvalue" . '<p>' ;
      $counter++;

}

?>


</body>
</html>
```

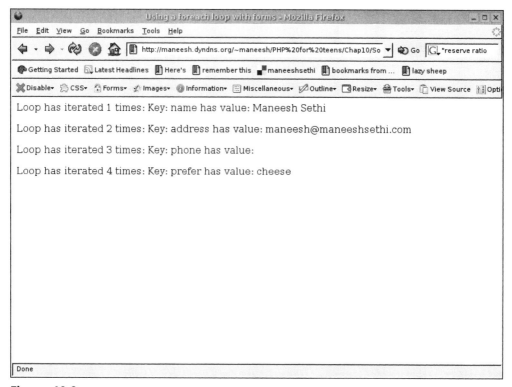

Figure 10.9
Displaying results in phpft10-06.php.

This ends up looking like Figure 10.9.

Whoa, look at that. The page displays the proper results by showing the key value and the real value of each element in the $_GET array. Remember that the $_GET array actually is a predefined container that holds all of the elements submitted through the GET method on a form. When we used the form on the last page, we sent all the information through GET to the new page. This page then took that data and looped through each element of the array, displaying the key value and the real value on the screen. With that, we got the results we wanted!

This program properly reports the value of every field of every form with a GET method. This form is not tied to a specific form, and you can use any HTML page to reference this PHP page, and it will display all the elements of your GET array. This is useful to check for errors. Pretty cool, huh?

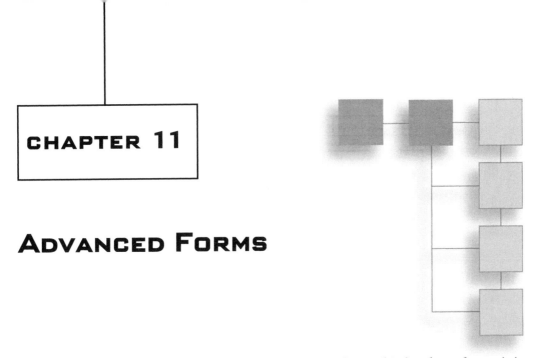

CHAPTER 11

ADVANCED FORMS

We've been using forms in almost every chapter so far in this book, and now it is time to learn more about what they can do. We have only been using basic forms so far, such as those with textboxes and a submit button or a selection box. In this chapter we take a closer look at web forms and see how PHP can make them very strong. I start by discussing some more-advanced HTML form elements, and then discuss the ways to use the forms in PHP to make your pages more robust.

Advanced Elements

Get ready—I go over a lot of different form elements in this chapter.

Radio Buttons

Radio buttons are organized into groups: Only one in a group of radio buttons can be selected. Use the <input> tag with the type set to radio (the same way that you do with a checkbox). However, you need to add one more parameter in addition to type and name: value. This parameter becomes the value of the $_GET or $_POST array that you access through PHP. For items of the same group, all of their name parameters are identical. This becomes the key of the GET or POST array.

It's important to note that a key/value pair is only sent if at least one of the radio buttons is selected. For this reason, if you decide to not make one of the radio buttons checked by default, make sure that the array key is set. If you don't test this, the user can simply skip the radio button section, creating an error when you try to access the radio button. You can ensure that at least one button was checked by using the $isset() function.

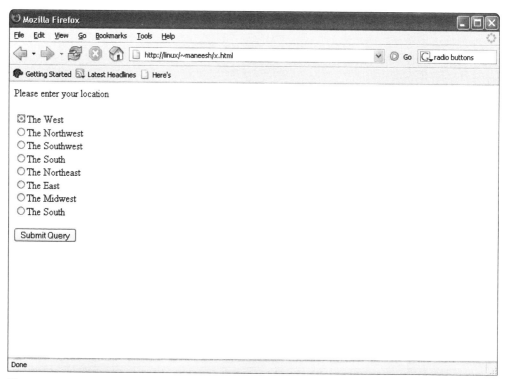

Figure 11.1
A sample set of radio buttons.

You might want to create a page that asks the user where he lives. This can be done with a simple set of checkboxes, like the ones that are in Figure 11.1.

As you can see in the figure, only one item is selected: the West (because I'm from California). If you click another, the West radio button clears and the other is selected. Let's look at the HTML code that makes this page possible:

```
<body>

Please enter your location

<form action="something.php" method="post">
<br /><input type="radio" name="location" value="west">The West
<br /><input type="radio" name="location" value"northwest">The Northwest
<br /><input type="radio" name="location" value"southwest">The Southwest
<br /><input type="radio" name="location" value"south">The South
```

```
<br /><input type="radio" name="location" value"northeast">The Northeast
<br /><input type="radio" name="location" value"east">The East
<br /><input type="radio" name="location" value"midwest">The Midwest
<br /><input type="radio" name="location" value"south">The South

<p><input type="submit">

</form>
</body>
```

Notice how all of the buttons have the same name? That is because this parameter defines which group they are in. If you had changed half of them to have a different name, you could select two items, one from each group. Figure 11.2 shows how this would happen if I had changed this into two groups. As you can see, two buttons have been selected. That is because the items have a different value for name. In Figure 11.2, all I did was change the name of the second group.

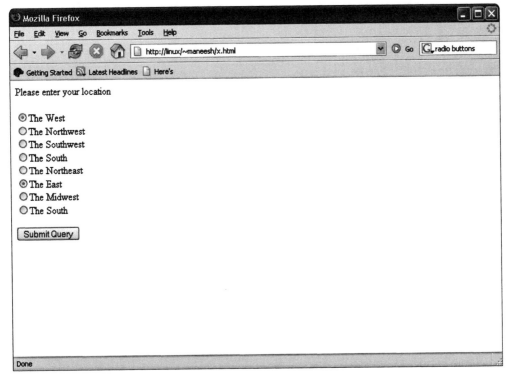

Figure 11.2
Splitting the radio buttons into two groups.

Password Fields

A *password field* is very simple. It looks identical to a textbox, except that the characters are *coded,* or hidden, from view. They look like asterisks or dots, depending on your browser. A password box is most commonly used when you want the user to be able to log into your site and is often used in conjunction with a username field. When typing in a password box, you get a result that looks like Figure 11.3. The code for this page follows.

```
<body>

Please enter in your username and password to log in.
<form action="something.php" method="post">
<p>Username:<input type="text" name="username">
<p>Password:<input type="password" name="password">

<p><input type="submit">

</form>
</body>
```

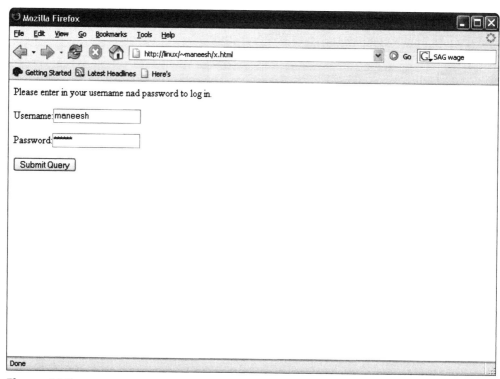

Figure 11.3
Using a password box.

Caution

A password box does not secure or encrypt the data in any way, so it is possible the information could be stolen.

Remember to use the POST method on your form. GET sends the data through the address bar, and it is very easy to steal the data just by looking at the URL. POST hides this data from the link. If you send data through POST, make sure you use the $_POST array to access data.

Note

I go over file selectors, another important HTML element, in Chapter 14.

Hidden Fields

Another type you might want to learn about is the hidden field. No user can see it, but a *hidden field* can pass data through forms. You can use the hidden field to keep necessary data alive through all of your pages in a simple manner. You can make a hidden field like follows:

```
<input name="hiddenfield" type="hidden" value="whateverValueYouWant" />
```

Using PHP and Forms

So far we have looked at the basics of entering items on a form and submitting it to another page that utilizes PHP and deals with the inputs. However, you may not want to have to submit the information to another page. In cases like this you can have the PHP form submit the data to itself: The same page that loads takes in the data and uses it for calculations. This can be useful when you want the user's input to change the page onscreen.

I have used this myself when developing a web site. On one page, the user was allowed to enter a code to make the item cheaper. I didn't want the page to submit the code data to another page, because that would require multiple pages with almost entirely identical content. Instead, I developed only one page that dealt with the data if the coupon code was submitted, but hid the PHP if the code was skipped.

The first thing I needed to do was develop a form. In most cases, the form submits the data to another page using the action attribute, but in this case we did not have the benefit of having another page to submit the information. Fortunately, there is a predefined variable that contains the address of the page from where it is called. This is part of the predefined array $_SERVER and the complete variable name is $_SERVER['PHP_SELF']. By setting the action attribute of the <form> tag to this location, the form sent the data to the same page and interacted upon it. The form declaration looked something like this:

```
<form name="couponcode" action="<?php $_SERVER['PHP_SELF'] ?>" method="get">
//rest of form here
</form>
```

Note

There is an easier way to do this, if you remember from earlier chapters. By leaving out the action attribute altogether, the form will call itself automatically. However, I wanted to demonstrate some cool interpolation and array variables, so we will continue with $_SERVER['PHP_SELF'] for this example.

Check out the action attribute. This wants to use the PHP_SELF variable, but the problem is that HTML itself does not know what the variable means! Only PHP uses this predefined variable, so we need to escape into PHP before using the array variable. This is done using <?php and ?>.

Now that we have created the basic level of the form, we need to add a textbox that allows the user to enter a coupon code. The textbox is very simple and allows regular letters and numbers.

```
Please enter in your coupon code <input type="text" name="couponcode" />
<input type="submit">
```

This creates the basic coupon code outline in which the user can type the code and press the submit button. If we wrote the form correctly, the page should simply refresh. We have created a form whose action is itself, but has no data to pass on and no way to interact with that data.

We need to write some actual PHP to handle anything that might come up. To do this, we are going to add the code before the form. The code we need to write might look something like the following:

```
<?php
$code = $_GET['couponcode'];

echo "You entered the coupon code " . $code;

?>
```

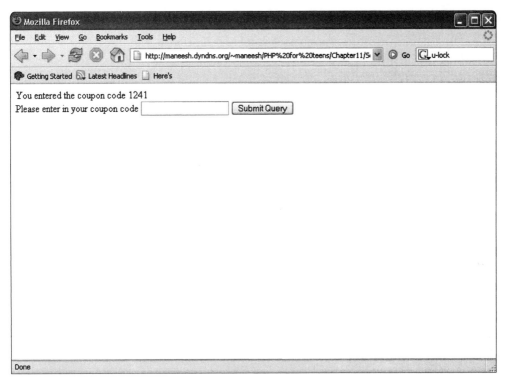

Figure 11.4
Beginning to use a coupon code.

Let's put this code together. The result is shown in Figure 11.4. You can find this file on the CD as `phpft11-01.php`. This looks pretty normal, right? As soon as you submit the data, the coupon code appears. However, what happens if you don't submit something? What happens if you just load the page? Check out Figure 11.5.

Uh oh. In this case, it just left the document blank. That is because the PHP code will always display the text `"You entered the coupon code"`, whether or not there is a code to show. Let's fix this problem. We need to add some data to make the text show only when a code has actually been submitted. Our page will probably end up looking like the following, the way it does in `phpft11-02.php`:

```
<!DOCTYPE html PUBLIC "-//W3C//DTD XHTML 1.0 Strict//EN"
    "http://www.w3.org/TR/xhtml1/DTD/xhtml1-strict.dtd">


<html>
<body>
```

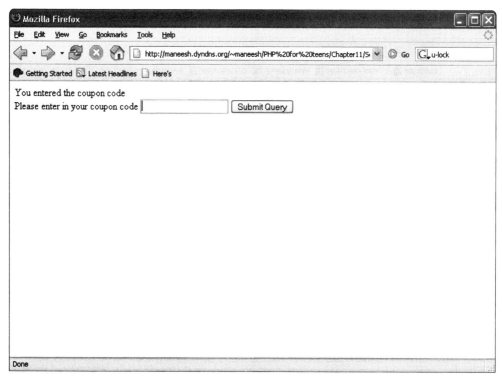

Figure 11.5
Using the code without submitting the form.

```php
<?php
$code = $_GET['couponcode'];

if (empty($code)){
?>
      <form name=.couponcode. action="<?php $_SERVER['PHP_SELF'] ?>"
method="get">

      Please enter in your coupon code <input type=.text. name="couponcode" />
      <input type="submit">

<?php
}
else
{
      echo "You entered the coupon code $code";

}
?>
```

```
</form>

</body>
</html>
```

Now check out what happens when you load up the page. See Figure 11.6.

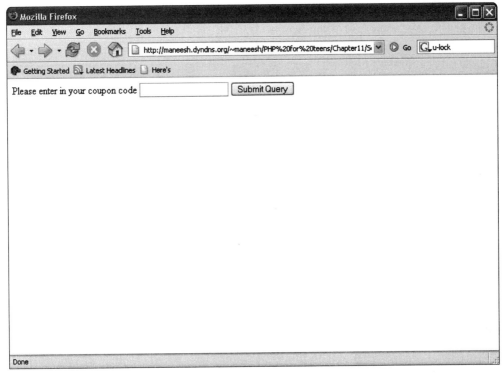

Figure 11.6
The coupon code form in `phpft11-02.php` without data.

All right! If you want to have a form submit data to the same page, so that any input is reflected on itself, this is how you do it!

We used kind of a cool trick. When using conditional statements in PHP, anything between the condition is executed only if the condition is `true`. That means that after the test `if`, the HTML form is only shown if the `empty` condition is true. Even though we exited PHP using the `?>` symbol, the `if` statement still stands: Anything inside is only executed if the statement is true. Also, we used a new function: `empty()`. This function is true is the variable is blank, and has no data inside of it.

By the way, in most cases with items like this, you only want the code to change the page if it is identical to a predefined number. Most codes are useless if they just write themselves on the same page.

To do a comparison, just compare the code to a predefined number. If they match, change the page as you like. Look at phpft11-03.php, which is on the CD:

```
<body>

<form name="code" action="<?php echo $_SERVER['PHP_SELF']; ?>" method="get">
<p>For the purposes of this page, the code is 31413. Try entering in this number
   and other numbers.
<p>Please enter in your coupon code:  <input type="text" name="couponcode" />
<p>

<?php

$code = $_GET['couponcode'];

if ($code == '31413')
        {
        echo "<font color=red>Congratulations, you have the code!</font><p>";
        }

?>
<input type="submit">

</form>

</body>
```

For this page, we moved the PHP section down near the end, after the input button. We set the variable so that if $code equals the specific constant we are looking for, a special text value is echoed to the screen. If the value is incorrect, the statement is never echoed. Check out what the page looks like in Figure 11.7.

Basic Email Commands

If you wish to send email through an HTML form, a very simple method is to use the mail() function built into PHP. Mail() gives the ability to send out a very basic email with a to address filled in. In addition, you can have a subject and a message inside the email. Let's look at a basic email declaration.

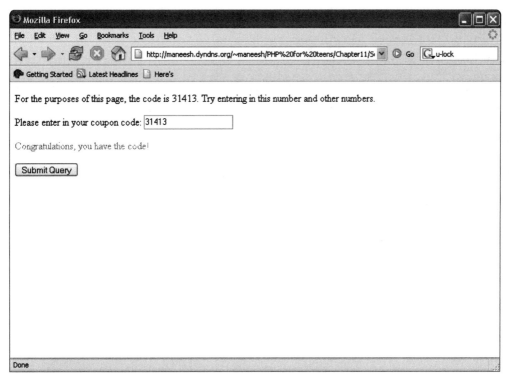

Figure 11.7
Changing the code in `phpft11-03.php`.

Notice that it seems like you cannot choose to change who the message is from. Actually, you can. Just choose one of these methods:

- Define it manually within the `$additionalheaders` variable.

- Go into your `php.ini` file from your PHP installation and configure the `from` address directly in the file.

Because the web server is handling part of the sending, the `from` option on the email will be from the web server.

Note

The web server is not actually sending the email. PHP uses an external program to send mail. In most cases, this function won't work after installing on Windows, unless you do some extra configuration. You can find out more about how to configure your server for sending email on `www.php.net` or `www.maneeshsethi.com`.

We are going to create one basic form that lets you enter a message, a subject, and a from and to address. We will put that into a PHP mailer and let the file email something to whomever the user chooses. Let's start off by designing the form document. This file is located in phpft11-04.html on the CD.

```
<!DOCTYPE html PUBLIC "-//W3C//DTD XHTML 1.0 Strict//EN"
    "http://www.w3.org/TR/xhtml1/DTD/xhtml1-strict.dtd">

<html>
<head>
<title>PHP Email</title>
</head>

<body>
<form name="email" action=phpft11-04.php method="post">

<p>Please fill out the form to send an email.
<p>Enter your email address: <input type="text" name="from"> Enter recipient's
email address: <input type="text" name="to">
<p>Enter subject: <input type="text" name="subject">
<p>Enter your message:<br> <textarea name="message" rows=10 cols=40>
  </textarea>

<p><input type="submit"> <input type="reset">
</form>

</body>

</html>
```

This is a pretty simple page, right? You can see what it looks like in Figure 11.8.

If you thought this was simple, look at the PHP code you send it in phpft11-04.php:

```
<?php
$to      = $_POST['to'];
$subject = $_POST['subject'];
$message = $_POST['message'];
$headers = 'From: ' . $_GET['from'] . "\r\n" .

mail($to, $subject, $message, $headers);
?>
```

Figure 11.8
The mail form in `phpft11-04.html`.

This page takes in all the necessary prerequisites for sending out an email and organizes them into a `mail()` function. Look closely at the `$headers` section: Be careful with that. The `$from` variable has to be formulated in a special way: `'From: emailaddress.'`. The extra `\r\n` allows you to later add headers, such as `Reply-To`. By doing this, we have now sent out an email to whoever is in the `$to` textbox! Pretty cool, huh?

You can use this on your web sites if you want to give the user a way to email you. I have a very similar script set up on my web site, which allows users to subscribe to my forum by way of email. You can probably think of many more uses for email technology.

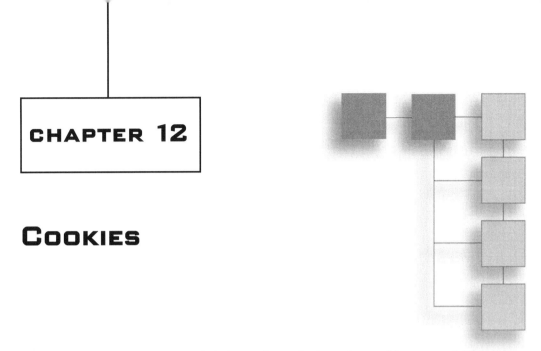

CHAPTER 12

COOKIES

PHP has many functions and abilities for web sites. One of these capabilities is to create and use cookies. You may have heard of cookies while using your web browser. A *cookie* is a text file stored on the user's machine. This text file has a data value, which stores some small amount of data. You just load this text file as a variable on pages that use the cookie, and that is your stored data! The text file is stored, in a hidden spot, by your web browser.

Basically, a cookie is a way for a site to save some data on your computer. This can be good and bad. For example, a lot of spyware sites use cookies to keep track of where you visit and use this data to sell ads to you. Also, make sure you don't overdo it: A lot of people don't like a lot of cookies because it can seem like you are storing data about them. On the other hand, using cookies allows you to choose and have those choices reflected on the site every time you use it.

This might seem vague, so let me give an example. Say you have a site where the user enters her name. This name might be reflected in many parts of the site, such as on the top of every page and in printable sections and documents. It is a little annoying to have to reenter her name every time the user enters the site, so adding cookies is a great way to make things a little easier. The Internet, as a whole, does not save data, so the developers of PHP came up with cookies.

Creating Cookies

Set cookies using the setcookie() function. This function has a lot of parameters.

```
setcookie($name, [$value, $expire, $path, $domain, $secure])
```

What do those brackets ([]) in the function declaration mean? Take a look at the setcookie() function. When a parameter is enclosed by brackets in a declaration like this, the parameters are optional. If you would prefer to leave them as they are by default, you can do that. In addition, be careful when defining only some of the default values. If you want to change the $secure parameter, but not the $path parameter, you still have to set $path. This is because you can only set the parameters from left to right—you cannot skip any. You must set $name first, $value second, $expire third, and so on. If you want to set one of the later parameters, you can set the earlier ones to their default value.

$name

The first parameter of setcookie() is $name. This is the name of the cookie, and you will use this to reference it in the future. In fact, the cookie eventually becomes part of an array called $_COOKIE, so if you want to reference a cookie, you would do it by calling the array like this:

```
$_COOKIE['name'];
```

As you can see, the name eventually becomes its key for the array that it is a part of.

$value

The function's second parameter is $value. If you want the cookie to be of any real use, you need to give it a value. You can reference the cookie later, get the value back, and use this value to affect your web site. In the example at the beginning of the chapter, we talked about creating a cookie that had a value of the visitor's name. We would store the value using the $value parameter. We could then pull this value back later, and use it to reference the visitor's name throughout the web site.

$expire

$expire is the first complex parameter, because it isn't part of the basic name-and-value entity. Instead, it refers to the amount of time, in seconds, that the cookie should remain on the server. By default, if you leave the $expire parameter blank, the cookie disappears as soon as the visitor closes his browser. By setting $expire, you can make the cookie last a lot longer.

Having a cookie run for the default amount of time—until the browser closes— is rarely useful in practice. If you were designing the page that remembers the user's name, it would be ridiculous for it only to remember the name for one session. Using the $expire attribute allows the cookie to last for a meaningful length of time. However, in pages where you only want the cookie to last throughout the current use of the browser, you can use the cookie without the $expire attribute.

To set the time, we need a new function: time(). For the technical minded, this function returns the number of seconds since the *epoch* (which is an arbitrary point in time; most computers use January 1, 1970 as the epoch), but you can just think of it as returning what time it is now. You set $expire to the value of time() plus the number of seconds you want the function to expire in.

Let's see how we could define the time. We need the function to expire in a set period of days or weeks. We can use the following $expire code:

```
$expire = time() + 60 * 60 * 24 * 30
```

Assuming we created the variables correctly earlier, this is identical to the following:

```
$expire = time() + $secondsPerMinute * $minutesPerHour * $hoursPerDay *
  $daysPerMonth;
```

Hmm, so what does this do? Remember that time() returns the current time in seconds. We want to add the number of seconds we want the cookie to endure to the current time. If we forget to add time(), the cookie will have expired several decades ago, making it worthless.

Here are some cool examples of time. This isn't actual PHP code, but it demonstrates how you can use time().

```
15 seconds = time() + 15;
30 minutes = time() 60 * 30
5 hours = time() * 60 * 60 * 5
10 days = time() * 60 * 60 * 24 * 10
```

Now that we have added the current time, we want to add the amount of time the cookie should last. Using multiplication like this makes it a lot easier to understand. The first 60 is measured in seconds/minute, times 60 minutes/hour, times 24 hours/day, times 30 days. This will result in a cookie that expires after 30 days. If we wanted to change it so that the cookie expired after two weeks, we could do something like this:

```
$name = "samplecookie";
$value= "samplevalue";
$expire= time() + 60 * 60 * 24 * 14; //expire in 2 weeks
setcookie($name, $value, $expire);
```

This creates a cookie with the key samplecookie and the value samplevalue to expire after 14 days.

The following setcookie() parameters are optional. You can use them when you want your cookies to work in specific cases or be stored in specific locations.

$path

The $path variable lets you choose the path of the web server on which the cookie will be valid. The default value is the directory that the file is in. You can make the cookie valid for all the pages in your web server by setting $path to /. If you set it to /somefolder/images, the cookie only works in the images folder of somefolder. Make sure you set the correct path so you can use your cookies in all the pages you want for your site.

$domain

$domain is most often used when you have a web site with several subdomains. A *subdomain* is a site that is a part of the original site, but whose URL is separated by a period. For example, maneeshsethi.com is the original site. I might create a subdomain such as subdomain.maneeshsethi.com. The actual domain is maneeshsethi.com, and the subdomain is subdomain.maneeshsethi.com. One trick here is to remember that www.maneeshsethi.com is considered a subdomain of maneeshsethi.com. Even the www makes the site into a subdomain.

$domain refers to the domain for which the cookie is valid. In most cases, you want it to be valid for your entire web site. This is common when you have a site that people might visit at website.com and at www.website.com. Because www.website.com is considered a subdomain, make sure that the cookie is valid for both options.

To make the cookie valid to all subdomains, make the cookie set to `.website.com`, with a period before the name. This causes all subdomains to recognize the cookie. If you want only `www.website.com` to accept the cookie, use `www.website.com` as your `$domain`.

$secure

The `$secure` parameter indicates that the cookie should only work over a secure HTTPS connection. We have not gone over HTTPS for this book, so it will not work if you set this Boolean parameter to `true`. However, if you ever learn how to use HTTPS on your own, this is how you would enable it for your cookies.

Common Problems

Many people have some difficulty defining a cookie. Let's look at some of these problems.

- The web script in the PHP document does not recognize the cookie. Cookies are not usable until the web page has been refreshed, so if you try to use a cookie on the same page where you created the cookie, the cookie will not work. In cases like these, simply use the value you assigned to the cookie to the areas where the value was going to be used.

- The web browser accessing the document has disallowed cookies on the page. This causes a problem creating a cookie and throws out any you create. Double-check that your page will work well without cookies if a user wants to use the page without them.

- Sometimes, developers try to create a cookie that has no value. That is fine, but make sure you set the value to " (no value), not false. Using the Boolean false creates a cookie that automatically deletes itself. Use a regular cookie and leave the value blank. A cookie with no value could let your PHP script know that the user has visited there before, sort of as a place mark.

- Cookies change the HTTP header, so you cannot put the `setCookie` function that defines and deletes cookies after any HTML code. Make sure your cookie code goes before the HTML header.

If you double-check, your pages should be fine.

Putting a Cookie in Your Site

Now it is time to put your knowledge into action. We are going to develop a couple pages with cookies, starting off with the one described earlier, which allows the user to enter a name on the form, which the web page remembers for a long period of time. The first thing we need to do is develop an HTML document. This HTML form allows the user to enter his name. From there, we will develop a couple of PHP forms that display the user's name.

```
<!DOCTYPE html PUBLIC "-//W3C//DTD XHTML 1.0 Strict//EN"
    "http://www.w3.org/TR/xhtml1/DTD/xhtml1-strict.dtd">
<html>
<head>
<title>Developing a page with cookies</title>
</head>

<body>
Please enter your name into the following text box and hit submit. Note that if
    you have entered in a name in the past few weeks, that name will be deleted with
    the new one.
<p>
<form name="cookie" action="phpft12-01.php" method="post">
Enter your name here:
<input type="text" name="name" />
<p>
<input type="submit" />
</form>

</body>
</html>
```

This is a very simple page, with just an input textbox. The page ends up looking like Figure 12.1. You can see this file on the CD as phpft12-01.html.

Let's enter a name in that box. You press submit, and what do you get? Nothing yet, because we still need to design the PHP page. Let's do that now. We want this PHP acceptor to do a couple of things:

- ▪ It should confirm whether a cookie has been created recently. If it has, then we need to delete that cookie and reset it with the new value. If not, it simply needs to create the new cookie.

■ It should direct the user to a new page, which shows the cookie results. If the cookie is valid, it will say the user's name; if invalid, the page will say that a cookie has not been set.

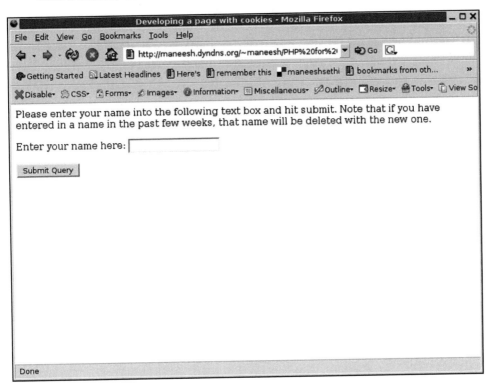

Figure 12.1
The `phpft12-01.html` file.

The PHP page is a little complex, so let's go through it one step at a time. Then, we will look it over all at once so you can see how everything flows. The first part of the script tests to see if the user left the field from the form page blank or did not access the PHP page through the form:

```php
<?php
$cookievalue = $_POST['name'];

//if cookievalue is blank, end the page
if ($cookievalue == '')
    {
        echo "You did not submit a cookie value. Please go back to
<a href=\"phpft12-01.html\"> phpft12-01.html</a> and correct this error.";
        exit;
    }
```

This section assigns the value of the form to the variable $cookievalue. It then tests to make sure $cookievalue has a value. If it is blank, a statement is echoed referring the user to go back to the form page and submit the form.

Note the following statement: exit. It uses a language construct exit. This construct should be used if there is an error—it halts execution of the PHP script in the web page and causes the page to skip over any further PHP. When you have an error such as this one, you can use exit to tell the browser that an error has occurred.

It's important to note that some PHP programmers prefer that you never use exit(), because it breaks the flow of the program. If you want the web page to completely load whether or not there is an error, you should not use exit(). The best time to use exit() is when the error is fatal, and you do not want the program to continue to execute without it.

After this section, we have another that checks to see if a cookie has been set recently, depending on the cookie length:

```
//If the cookie has been set recently
if (isset($_COOKIE['name']))
    {
        setCookie("name", "", time()-1);
      unset($_COOKIE['name']);
    }
```

Here, we use two new functions to see if a cookie has been created. isset() returns true if its parameter (in this case, the name cookie) has been set. If the cookie was set, we delete the cookie by resetting it to expire in the past, and then we use the unset() function to delete the cookie from the $_COOKIES array. Why do we reset the cookie with the setCookie() function? We have to redefine the cookie to delete it, because no function directly deletes it. Instead, we use the setCookie() function to delete it by creating a cookie with the same name that expires in the past (time()-1). The cookie is automatically deleted by the web browser.

The last step is to create the cookie:

```
//Whether or not the cookie was set earlier, set this cookie.
setcookie("name", $cookievalue, time() + 60 * 60 * 24 * 12);

echo "Cookie has been set, please visit
<a href=\"phpft12-01result.php\">phpft12-01result.php</a> to see the result.";

?>
```

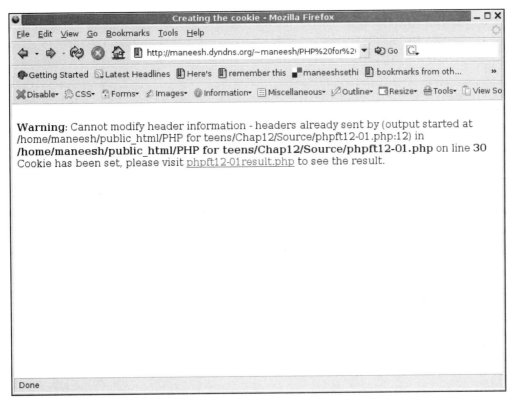

Figure 12.2
An error with the `phpft12-02.php` file.

We set the cookie to last 12 days by giving it an expire time of `time() + 60 * 60 * 24 * 12`, and we set the value to the name that was submitted on the form. Remember that you are creating stored bits of data that exist for a set amount of time, so the amount of time we use for the cookies is the time the cookie will exist.

Now, we put this in the web document after the `<body>` tag, and the script should execute flawlessly, right? Check out what happens when we do this by looking at Figure 12.2.

Uh oh. We got an error! What happened? When creating cookies, you have to put the cookie before any HTML tag. Cookies are part of a special part of the document which is dealt with before even the `<html>` tag. You need to set them before even the opening `<html>` tag. If you have any `<!DOCTYPE>` or `<meta>` tags, the cookie must go before these, also. This means that you cannot create a cookie after any executed `echo` statement in your program.

By rearranging the document so it looks like the following, we can get a better result:

```php
<?php

$cookievalue = $_POST['name'];
//if cookievalue is blank, end the page
if ($cookievalue == '')
    {
        echo "You did not submit a cookie value. Please go back to
<a href=\"phpft12-01.html\"> phpft12-01.html</a> and correct this error.";
        exit;
    }

//If the cookie has been set recently
if (isset($_COOKIE['name']))
    {
        unset($_COOKIE['name']);
    }

//Whether or not the cookie was set earlier, set this cookie.
setcookie("name", $cookievalue, time() + 60 * 60 * 24 * 12);

echo "Cookie has been set, please visit <a href=\"phpft12-01result.php\">
   phpft12-01result.php</a> to see the result.";

?>

<html>
<head>
<title>Creating the cookie</title>
</head>

<body>

</body>
</html>
```

We moved the PHP code above the <html> section. Notice that the body is empty. This doesn't matter: The cookie will still set and everything will work fine. Figure 12.3 shows the result.

Now all we have to do is create a simple PHP page that echoes out the cookie. This isn't too bad at all. Check out the following source from phpft12-01result. php on the CD:

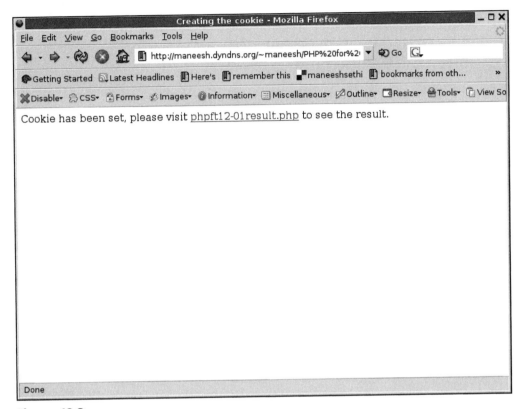

Figure 12.3
Finally setting a cookie in `phpft12-01.php`.

```
<!DOCTYPE html PUBLIC "-//W3C//DTD XHTML 1.0 Strict//EN"
    "http://www.w3.org/TR/xhtml1/DTD/xhtml1-strict.dtd">
<html>
<head>
<title>Displaying the cookie</title>
</head>

<body>

<?php

$cookievalue = $_COOKIE['name'];

//if the cookie is blank or does not exist, echo an error
if ($cookievalue == ")
    {
        echo "You have not created the cookie yet? Go to
<a href=\"phpft12-01.html\">phpft12-01.html</a> to set a cookie.";
```

```
        exit;
    }
else
    {
        echo "Welcome back to the page, $cookievalue. Feel free to change your
    cookie by visiting <a href=\"phpft12-01.html\">phpft12-01.html</a>.";
    }
?>
</body>
</html>
```

This page simply echoes an error if the cookie does not exist and displays the person's name if it does exist.

Let's see the three pages in succession. Figure 12.4 shows how a person can enter his name, Figure 12.5 shows the result of entering a name, and Figure 12.6 shows the final results.

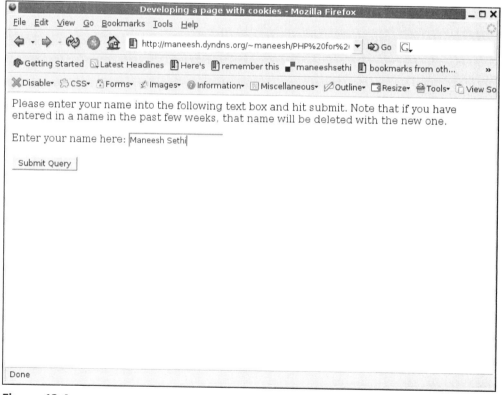

Figure 12.4
Step one: entering your name.

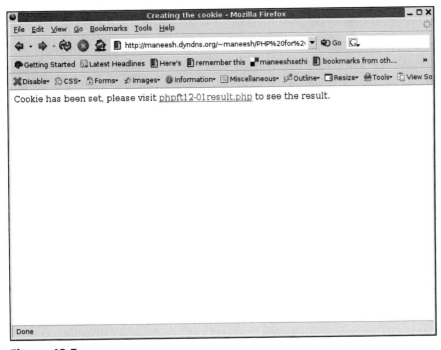

Figure 12.5
Step two: creating the cookie.

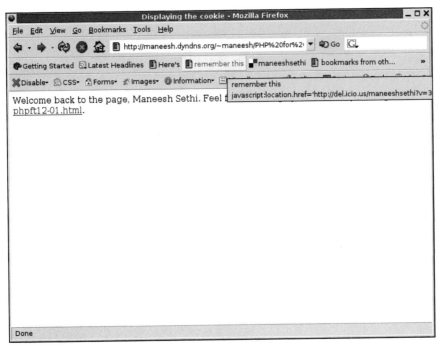

Figure 12.6
Step three: the results.

Check that out! Three steps to set a complete cookie and display it on one page.

I have an exercise for you: Rewrite these PHP pages so that it does all three of these steps on one page. Make one page display a form, set the cookie, and echo the result out if it exists. This is a pretty tough job, but I bet you are up to it!

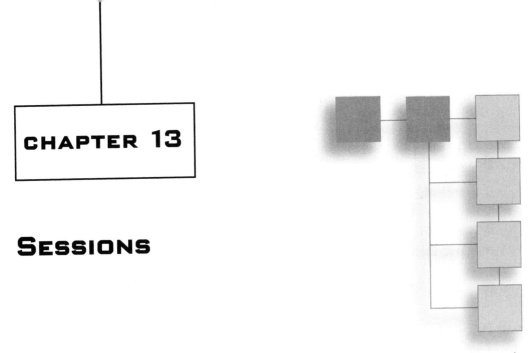

CHAPTER 13

SESSIONS

As you learned in Chapter 12, cookies allow you to save a small file, on the user's computer, that recorded some data in a variable. However, there are a few problems with saving data inside cookies for use in all your site's pages:

- Cookies are stored on the user's computer. This means that the user can go into the cookie file and edit the text to change the results of a page.

- Cookies are not super reliable. They can be turned off, deleted, and edited by hand, so you have to worry about what a knowledgeable user can do with cookies you create.

- A lot of Internet viewers don't like cookies, because they can track down visitors' locations and use them for advertising purposes. In fact, a lot of people on the Internet hate cookies for this reason, and they do not allow them altogether.

Because of all of these reasons, PHP created a completely new interface whenever you want to remember user data. This new interface is called a *session*. Sessions are very similar to cookies because they are another method of storing variables for use on a web site. However, there are several important differences between the two:

- Sessions store the variables on the server. This means that the user cannot edit any of the data that his computer uses because he cannot access it. In other words, sessions are a lot safer than cookies overall.

- Sessions cannot have an expiration time: They always expire as soon as the browser closes. Because no file is saved to the user's computer, the session variables simply lose their point of reference when the browser closes, and cannot be used anymore. Of course, you can find ways to get around this, but in most cases ending the session immediately is better for both the server and the user.

Sessions are a great way for implementing a username/password system on your website, and this chapter will discuss how to do that. We will also go over some other sample programs for which sessions are suited. Let's get started now.

Using Sessions

To start a session, you only need to use one function: `session_start()`. It automatically checks to see if a session is already running on your browser and, if not, assigns a new session ID. If a session is already running, it joins that session and uses it on the current page. A *session ID* is simply a sequence of numbers assigned to your computer when you start a session. Each computer gets a different session ID; it helps the web server keep track of who is doing what on the web site and inside the session.

`session_start()` must be placed before any other echoed HTML or test. This is exactly the same thing that happened with `setcookie()` in Chapter 12. Because sessions deal with the document header, the function pertaining to them must be placed right at the beginning. Figure 13.1 shows what happens if `session_start()` is placed after some text is echoed to the screen.

The code that produced this error is very short:

```
There will be an error below!
<?php
session_start();
?>
```

We entered `There will be an error below` on the screen. However, because we wrote *anything* on the screen, we got the following error:

```
session_start(): Cannot send session cookie - headers already sent
```

Why did we get this error? Sessions have to start in the header of a document, before anything at all is written on the screen. After the first piece of text or the

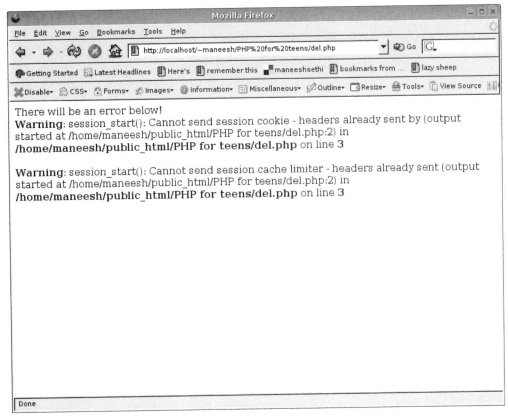

Figure 13.1
Producing an error with `session_start()`.

first HTML tag (including `<html>`) is written, the server header section is over, and `session_start` can no longer begin.

Starting a Session

Let's try changing the code just a little bit. The result is shown in Figure 13.2.

```php
<?php
session_start();
?>
Will there be an error above?
```

There is no error at all. Make sure that `session_start()` appears before any other text or HTML tags.

```php
header("Cache-control: private");
```

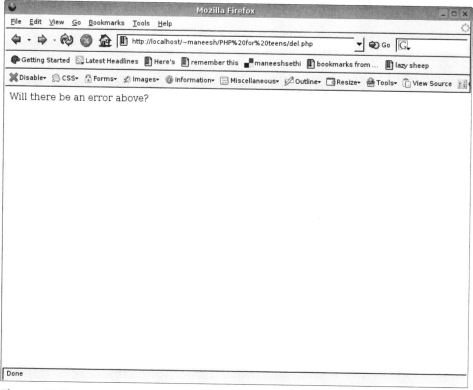

Figure 13.2
Fixing the error with `session_start()`.

We have started our session, so what's next? Let's try making a page similar to the one we made in Chapter 12, where the user can enter her name and have the page display the name onscreen. We will use sessions rather than cookies to achieve this, however.

Designing a Form Page

First of all, we need to design a form page. We are going to use a form identical to the one we made last chapter, which looks like Figure 13.3. Check out Chapter 12's code listing on the CD as `phpft13-01.html` or download the source from www.maneeshsethi.com.

Developing a Basic PHP Page

Now that we have a form set up, it's time to actually put our session to work! Let's start off by developing a basic PHP page that saves the user's name to a variable that crosses different pages.

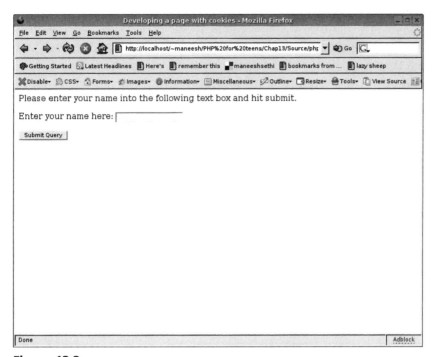

Figure 13.3
The `phpft13-01.html` file.

Our new page starts with the introductory section:

```php
<?php
session_start();
header("Cache-control:private");
```

Note that the form passed the name of the user using the POST method.

Now we need to assign a session variable to contain the value of the name that it passes. In other chapters you have seen the $_POST array, the $_GET array, and the $_COOKIE array. All of these valid arrays apply to their type of data. Take a guess what the session array is. You guessed it: $_SESSION.

We actually get to define the elements of the $_SESSION array ourselves. In the $_POST and $_GET arrays, the web server or the previous form sends the data to us, through the arrays. With $_SESSION, there is no data to download; instead, we create the array ourselves.

We are going to add an element to the array that lets us transfer some data across the session. We are going to create an element which stores the user's name. The following code fragment shows you how:

```php
$_SESSION['name'] = $_POST['name'];
```

Not too bad at all, eh? All we did was create a new element of the $_SESSION array and assign it to the form posted value of the $_POST array. By doing this, we have created a variable that persists throughout the session on any page that we use session_start() on. Basically, that is all we need to transfer the data. Let's add a text field just for good measure:

```
echo "Thanks for visiting the page {$_POST['name]}.
Your name has been added to the session variable list!
Visit <a href=\"phpft13-01result.php\" >phpft13-01result.php</a>
to see the result!"
?>
```

And now we have completely designed the page. Check out Figure 13.4 for the result. As you can see, we have added the session variable to the session list.

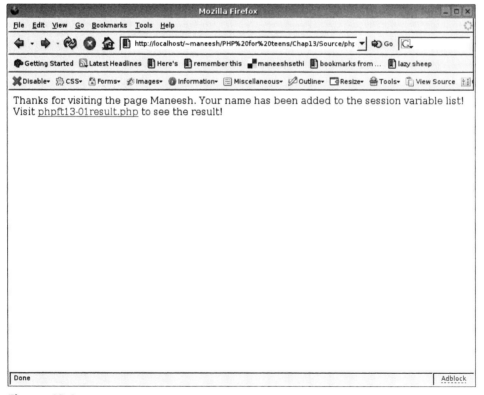

Figure 13.4
The phpft13-01.php file.

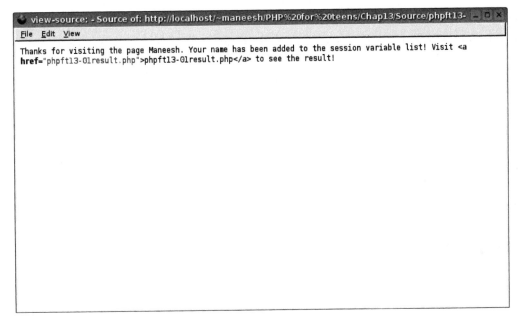

Figure 13.5
The source of the phpft13-01.php file.

We then displayed the correct message, and set the user up to look at the next page, which holds his variable. Look at the source in Figure 13.5. The PHP server translated that PHP code we wrote into simply a line of text with a link (<a href>). Not bad at all.

So now we have only one page left. Check out what this page looks like in Figure 13.6. Following is the code for the phpft13-01result file, which uses the stored session data to print the user's name:

```php
<?php
session_start();
header("Cache-control:private");

echo "Thanks for visiting our site, $_SESSION['name']. If your name appears in
  this document, sessions work correctly!";
?>
```

While we are at it, let's update the phpft13-01result.php file. We are going to have the file display all the session data it can handle. PHP has a bunch of

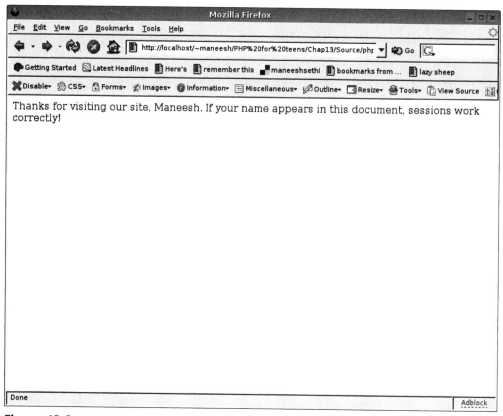

Figure 13.6
The `phpft13-01result.php` file.

functions for dealing with session data, and we are going to go over some of them now.

PHP Functions for Session Data

Sessions are great tools for passing variables on your web site, but there is a possible problem. You can get into trouble if two scripts use variables of the same name. When Programmer A develops his web page, he creates a form where the user can enter his information to ship an item. He calls this session variable `$name`. Programmer B, who is an amateur PHP developer, decides to create a page in which `$name` tracks the user's name. Well, if a visitor goes to the page developed by Programmer A, and then he goes to the second page developed by Programmer B, the `$name` variable is tracked and perhaps unchangeable. This can be a problem because we don't want both users getting mixed up without letting the user know that there was a mixup.

The Errored Pages

Before we go over the fix, let's develop a couple problem pages. The first page has a basic form for entering your email address.

```
<!DOCTYPE html PUBLIC "-//W3C//DTD XHTML 1.0 Strict//EN"
    "http://www.w3.org/TR/xhtml1/DTD/xhtml1-strict.dtd">
<html>
<head>
<title>A form demonstrating session name problems</title>
</head>

<body>
<form action="phpft13-02.php" method="get">
Please enter your email address: <input type="text" name="address">
<input type="submit">
</form>
</body>

</html>
```

Pretty run of the mill—a form with a submit button, like you see in Figure 13.7.

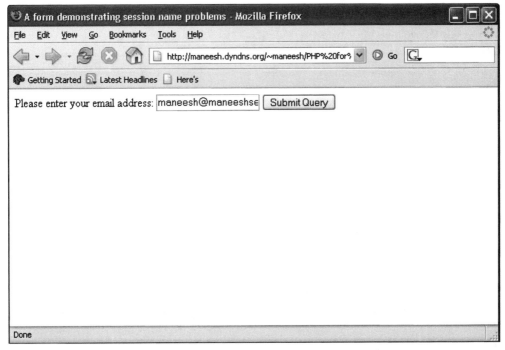

Figure 13.7
The phpft13-02.php file.

We are going to have it go to another simple web page that displays the email address after assigning it to a session. Here is another very simplistic web page, phpft13-02.php, which starts a session and assigns a session variable. See the result in Figure 13.8.

```php
<?php
session_start();
header("Cache-control:private");

$_SESSION['address'] = $_GET['address'];

echo "Thanks for visiting the page with the email address
  {$_SESSION['address']}. Your name has been added to the session variable list!
  Now, if everything is working correctly, this session variable should NOT work
  on <a href=\"phpft13-02other.php\">phpft13-02other.php</a>"
?>
```

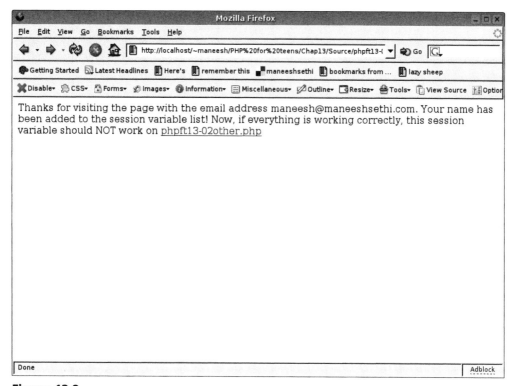

Figure 13.8
The phpft13-02.php file.

Okay, we got the expected result. Very good so far. Now here is the rub: We want to make a new page that uses an $address variable from another form. Assume the form has been created and that the user bypassed the form and opened the PHP document. In cases like this, the $address variable should be blank, right? Because we created a session with the variable, $address is passed along. Let's check out this error-filled document. It is on the CD as phpft13-02other.php.

```php
<?php
session_start();
header("Cache-control:private");

$address = $_SESSION['address'];

if ($address != '')
{
    echo "Uh oh, there is an error. \$address is registered.";
}
else
{
    echo "Great! \$address is unregistered as a session variable!";
}

?>
```

The Fix

This is a little different from what you have seen before, huh? We created an if. . .else section that tests to see whether the variable $address exists. The first test checks to make sure that $address is *not* blank. If it is not blank, then there is an error—the variable has carried through. If it is blank, then the session variable has not carried through and it works correctly.

Let's see what happens when you go to this page through your browser after creating a session variable from the earlier file. Check out the result in Figure 13.9. Uh oh! I got an error because the variable is registered. This is the problem we were expecting, and now we need to figure out a way to fix it.

Fortunately, the fix is simple: When dealing with sessions, each session has a *session name*. Any script that uses session_start() gets a default session name, and the script uses this session name to carry variables from page to page. However, if we want to differentiate two pages, we can create a new session name for the scripts, causing the variables not to carry through.

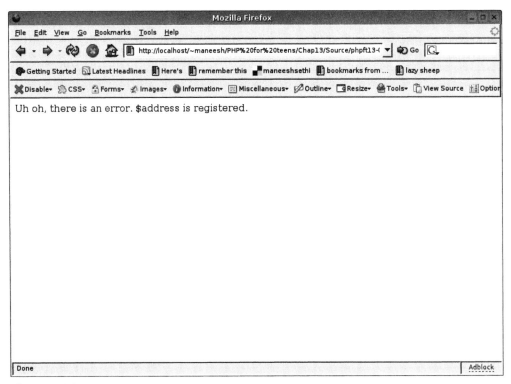

Figure 13.9
The `phpft13-02other.php` file.

Changing the session name is very simple. All you need to do is use the `session_name()` variable. Include a parameter of the name you wish to assign it, and there you go! One step to create a new session name. Note that the `session_name()` function must be placed before `session_start()`. You should use it at the beginning of your document, probably as the first line.

Let's rewrite the page to fix the problem. All we need to do is change the session name, and it should work.

```php
<?php
session_name("testname");
session_start();
header("Cache-control:private");

$address = $_SESSION['address'];

if ($address != '')
```

```
{
    echo "Uh oh, there is an error. \$address is registered.";
}
else
{
    echo "Great! \$address is unregistered as a session variable!";
    echo "<p>Our session name is " . session_name();
}

?>
```

This file is phpft13-03.php on the CD. Check out how it looks in Figure 13.10. Hey, check that out! The PHP document echoes the correct text because the new session name causes the session variable $address to be forgotten.

At the bottom of this script, I included an echo call that tells the current session name. If you use the session_name() function without any parameters, it returns

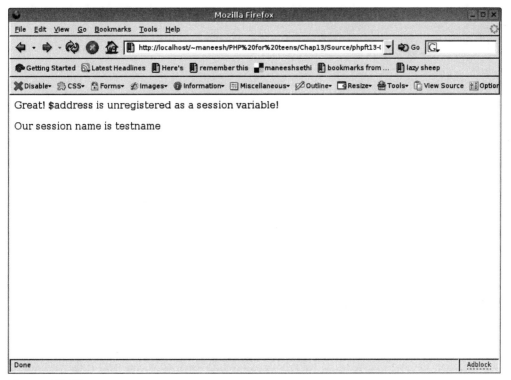

Figure 13.10
The phpft13-03.php file.

the current session name rather than applying a new session name. That is why this line echoed out the correct session name into the document:

```
echo "<p>Our session name is " . session_name();
```

All right, so now we know how to differentiate between sessions. This is a great way to allow different types of scripts on your pages without confusing the variables and getting them all mixed up.

Creating a Web Page Counter

Okay, let's try something new. Now that you know about basic session variables, let's create a web page counter. This counter will recognize how many times a visitor has visited your page and display the number on the screen. The counter starts at 0 when the page is closed.

Developing a counter requires just a little PHP. We will open a session and reference the counter (which creates the variable if it doesn't exist, or increments it if it does exist). The following code fragment is taken from phpft13-04.php:

```php
<?php
session_name("counter");
session_start();
header("Cache-control:private");

$_SESSION['counter']++;

echo "Hey, welcome to this web page. While you are here, feel free to browse
  some other sites. Just make sure you come back!. Hey, you might as well check
  out <a href=\"http://www.maneeshsethi.com\"> ManeeshSethi.com </a> while you
  are here!";

echo "<p>We will keep a record of how many times you come back!";

echo "<p><p><div align=\"center\">
You have visited our page {$_SESSION['counter']} times.";

?>
```

This is kind of strange, but all of the real power comes from this line:

```
$_SESSION['counter']++;
```

This line creates the counter variable if it does not exist, and it increments it by 1 using the ++ operator if it does exist. Then, we echo out the session counter at the bottom of the page. This tells the visitor how many times she has visited the site. When she leaves the page, the session remains open. If the user returns, the counter still increments correctly.

Let's see what happens. First of all, you open the session, as shown in Figure 13.11.

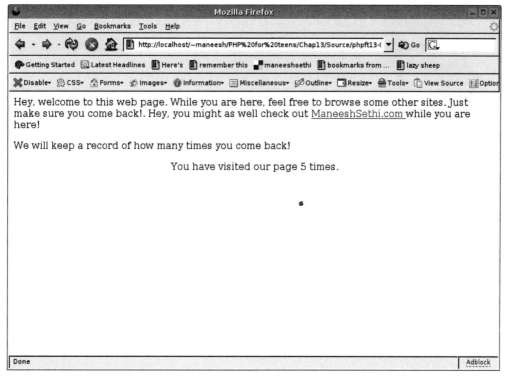

Figure 13.11
The phpft13-04.php file.

Now we are going to navigate away from the PHP page. We might go to the indicated site (www.maneeshsethi.com). Figure 13.12 shows how the PHP page has disappeared and has been replaced with ManeeshSethi.com.

Now go back to the PHP file. We cannot just press the browser's Back button, because we won't rerun the PHP script that way. Instead, we are going to access the correct file using the address bar. Type in the PHP file's location and check out the result in Figure 13.13. Check it out! The counter continues to update the

Figure 13.12
Navigating away from the PHP file.

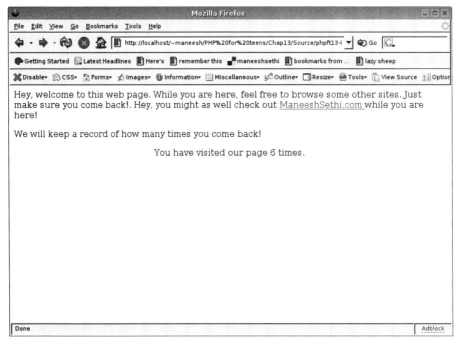

Figure 13.13
Returning to `phpft13-04.php`.

number even if the page has been changed! In Figure 13.11, you see a 5, and after leaving and coming back, the counter says 6.

If you want to keep the counter running even when the session ends, you could assign the value of the session variable to a cookie, and load the cookie every time the page runs. Why don't you try doing that as an exercise? We will come back to that program at the end of the chapter and create a running counter that tracks the visitor at all times. For right now, we are going to create a log-in page.

Developing a Log-In Page

Let's develop a web page that lets the user log in and log out. You have probably seen pages like this before: when you shop, post in forums, or bank online. Username and password forms are ubiquitous and very important, so it is a good thing to learn. In this section you learn the basics: a simple user/pass combination with different text strings for each user. You develop the user/pass script without any record-keeping abilities. (Remember that a password box is the same as a text box, except it disguises the entry with asterisks.)

The best way to create a user/pass section is to use a database. You can create new users by adding information into the database. To read about databases, I recommend *A Guide to SQL* by Philip J. Pratt and Mary Z. Last or *A Guide to MySQL* by Pratt (Course).

We are going to add two user accounts directly into our web page. The first user account will have the username test and the password test. The second user will have the username maneesh and the password password. First, we develop an HTML document that allows the visitor to log in. The following code is taken from phpft13-05.html and its results are in Figure 13.14:

```
<!DOCTYPE html PUBLIC "-//W3C//DTD XHTML 1.0 Strict//EN"
    "http://www.w3.org/TR/xhtml1/DTD/xhtml1-strict.dtd">
<html>
<head>
<title>Logging in using sessions</title>
</head>

<body>

<div align="center">Welcome to our session script. Please enter in your
  username and password.
```

```
<p>
<form name="session" action="phpft13-05.php" method="post">
Username:
<input type="text" name="user" />
<p>
Password;
<input type="password" name="pass" />
<p>
<input type="submit" />
</form>
</div>
<p><p>
Use these values if you do not have your own account.
<br>test/test
<br>maneesh/password

</body>
</html>
```

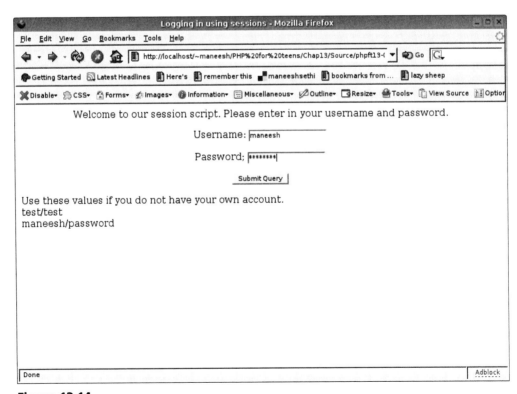

Figure 13.14
The phpft13-05.html file.

Hey, not bad looking. We have created a simple log-in form and told the user some of the options he can choose. So far, so good.

Before we move forward, I want to talk about the structure of our log-in PHP section. We have already created a form that allows the user to log in. The next page is going to be a little different than the form handlers we used in other chapters. Usually, we take in the information from the form and immediately act upon it or display it on the new PHP page. However, with a log-in form, we need to use one page to validate the user and confirm whether the information is correct. That means that the first page the form submits to simply checks the username and password. If they match one of the accounts, then it will register some variables for the account and move to another page that acts upon those variables. If the account is invalid, it displays an error and asks the user to log in again. Let's see the code for this PHP section:

```php
<?php
session_name("login");
session_start();

header("Cache-control:private");

$user=$_POST['user'];
$pass=$_POST['pass'];

//if the username/pass is blank, error
if ($user == '' || $pass == '')
{
    echo "ERROR: You must fill in both the username field and the password field.
Please push back on your browser and try again.";
    exit;
}

if ($user=='test' && $pass=='test')
{

    $_SESSION['name']="test";

    header("Location: http://" . $_SERVER['HTTP_HOST']
                        . rtrim(dirname($_SERVER['PHP_SELF']), '/\\')
                        . "/" . "phpft13-05loggedin.php");

    echo "Thank you for logging in test. You are being redirected to your account.";
```

```
}

elseif ($user=='maneesh' && $pass=='password')
{

        $_SESSION['name']="maneesh";

header("Location: http://" . $_SERVER['HTTP_HOST']
                        . rtrim(dirname($_SERVER['PHP_SELF']), '/\\')
                        . "/" . "phpft13-05loggedin.php");
    echo "Thank you for logging in, Maneesh. You are being redirected to your
account.";


}

else
{
echo "You have entered in an incorrect combination of username and password.
  Please try again.";
exit;
}



?>
```

That's pretty long! This page does a lot of complex things. The first few lines of code initiate the session and assign the username and password to local variables. After doing this basic, introductory stuff, the script begins to handle whatever was in the form.

The first if clause deals with a blank username or password field:

```
//if the username/pass is blank, error
if ($user == '' || $pass == '')
{
    echo "ERROR: You must fill in both the username field and the password
field. Please push back on your browser and try again.";
    exit;
}
```

Here, the $user and the $pass variables are checked. If either is blank, then an error has occurred. Note that || means *or,* so we are testing whether $user is blank *or* if $pass is blank. Figure 13.15 shows what happens if you leave one of the fields blank.

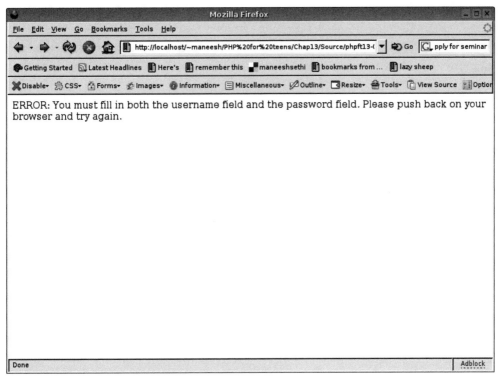

Figure 13.15
Leaving a field blank in the phpft13-05.php file.

The next if clause begins a series of ifs and else. . .ifs that work together to confirm whether the correct user has entered the information. The first test begins by checking if the user is the *test* user. The following is the snippet that tests:

```php
if ($user=='test' && $pass=='test')
{
    $_SESSION['name']="test";

    header("Location: http://" . $_SERVER['HTTP_HOST']
                        . rtrim(dirname($_SERVER['PHP_SELF']), '/\\')
                        . "/" . "phpft13-05loggedin.php");

    echo "Thank you for logging in test. You are being redirected to your account.";

}
```

The test begins by checking to see if the visitor entered test as both the username *and* the password (&& means *and*). If so, it begins by creating a new session variable: name. We pass it as a session variable and then must write a function that changes the user's location to a new page to deal with the information and the new variables.

To change the user's URL, we use header(). This function changes some sections of a document's header. In our case, we want the user to visit a new page if he logs in correctly. Therefore, we changed the header's Location attribute. You might have noticed how complex the header variable is. In fact, if we want to send the user to an absolute web site, such as www.cnn.com, the location header makes a lot more sense. This is how we would send a user to cnn.com:

```
header("Location: http://www.cnn.com");
```

However, header() only works with absolute web sites—you cannot send the user to a relative path such as newpage.html. You would have to send the user to http://localhost/newpage.html. Because you don't always have an absolute location of a web page's location, using an absolute header can be a real pain. Fortunately, several variables can create an absolute header out of a relative one.

Take a look at the preceding code. We take http:// and append the variable $_SERVER['HTTP_HOST'] to it. This variable is the beginning part of your domain, such as maneeshsethi.com or localhost. We then append a pretty complex section to this: rtrim(dirname($_SERVER['PHP_SELF']), '/\\'). We have seen the $_SERVER['PHP_SELF'] variable before, which is the file's identical location. The two functions that act upon it, rtrim() and dirname(), delete the self location and return to the previous folder. For example, if we were passing http://localhost/~user/php/text.html, using rtrim() and dirname() would result in ~user/php. We append ~user/php to the earlier section and get http://localhost/~user/php. The last step is to add the document we want the user to go to. Do this by adding a / and the filename.

All right! We have redirected a user to a new location. Our last step is to echo out some text telling the user that we are redirecting his location:

```
    echo "Thank you for logging in test. You are being redirected to your
account.";
```

The header() function is very quick, and in most cases the user won't even notice this text. However, if he has a particularly slow Internet connection, he may see this page. Figure 13.16 shows what this page looks like.

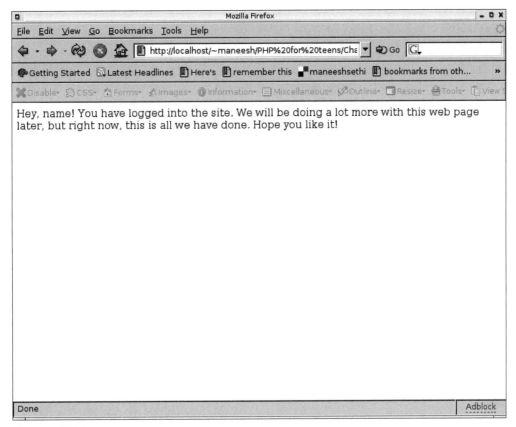

Figure 13.16
The phpft13-05.php file after logging in as test.

The program's next section does the same thing if the user logs in as maneesh. The only difference is that the passed $_SESSION['name'] variable is maneesh rather than test.

The last section of the if. . .else clause is executed only if the user enters an incorrect username and password:

```
else
{
echo "You have entered in an incorrect combination of username and password.
  Please try again.";
exit;
}
```

This section simply echoes out an error if either the username or password is incorrect, but both have been filled. The result looks like Figure 13.17.

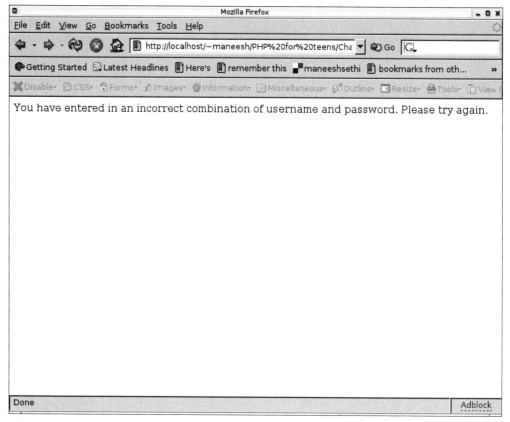

Figure 13.17
The `phpft13-05.php` file after logging in with an incorrect username or password.

We need to create a simple page that recognizes the user depending on the session variable. We do this in `phpft13-05loggedin.php`, which takes the session variables, which were created by logging in to the account, and reflects them on the final page. Check out the following code listing to see how it works:

```php
<?php
session_name("login");
session_start();

header("Cache-control:private");

$name = $_SESSION['name'];

echo "Hey, $name! You have logged into the site. We will be doing a lot more
  with this web page later, but right now, this is all we have done. Hope you
  like it!";

?>
```

This isn't too difficult, eh? We just created a page that echoes out the user's logged in name. Check out how it looks in Figure 13.18.

All right, we have created a complete login script! Granted, it doesn't do much, but we can make it a lot better when we save files to the server (which you learn about in Chapter 14).

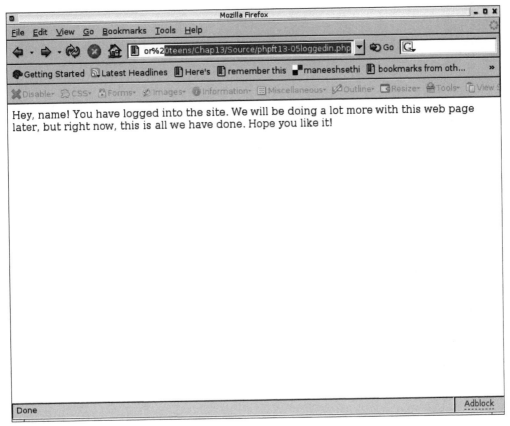

Figure 13.18
The `phpft13-05loggedin.php` page.

Cookie Exercise

Before leaving this chapter, let's go over the exercise regarding using cookies and a session in conjunction with each other to create a counter that always updates itself, even after the session has been ended and the browser has been closed. We are going to do this exercise by adding and updating a cookie every time the user visits the site. The following code answers this problem. Take a look and see if you can understand it all the way through without looking at the explanation.

```php
<?php
session_name("counter");
session_start();
header("Cache-control:private");

$_SESSION['counter'] = $_COOKIE['counter'];

$_SESSION['counter']++;

setcookie("counter", $_SESSION['counter'], time()+ 60 * 60 * 24 * 30);

echo "Hey, welcome to this web page. While you are here, feel free to browse
   some other sites. Just make sure you come back!. Hey, you might as well check
out <a href=\"http://www.maneeshsethi.com\"> ManeeshSethi.com </a> while you
   are here!";

echo "<p>We will keep a record of how many times you come back!";

echo "<p><p><div align=\"center\">You have visited our page
{$_SESSION['counter']} times.";

?>
```

This page uses cookies and sessions in conjunction to create a counter that remembers how many times you have visited the site even after you close the page! The page begins by setting up the session and assigning a session variable to the cookie variable. If the cookie variable does not exist, the session variable is assigned to 0. You might be wondering how the variable knows how to set the cookie variable to 0. If the variable does not exist, it automatically has a value of 0. This line performs that feat:

```php
$_SESSION['counter'] = $_COOKIE['counter'];
```

The next line increments the `$_SESSION['counter']` variable, updating the counter. Use this value for all future calculations in the script; it has the most updated counter value.

Next is the main line: It sets the cookie that recalls the value every time we load the page. The cookie has several important parameters, so take a look at the line of code:

```php
setcookie("counter", $_SESSION['counter'], time()+ 60 * 60 * 24 * 30);
```

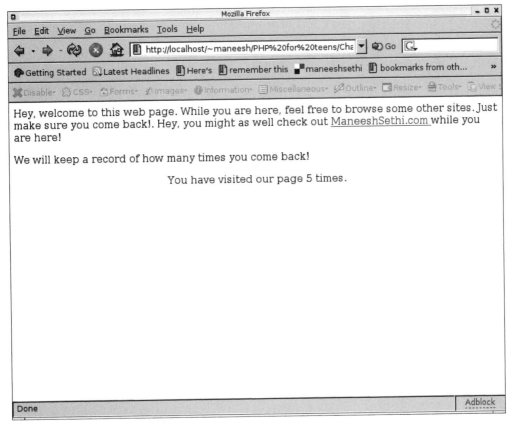

Figure 13.19
The `phpft13-06.php` counter page.

The first parameter is the cookie name. We used it in one of the earlier assigning lines of code. The second parameter is the cookie value. Notice that was the counter's `$_SESSION` value rather than the cookie value. This is because we updated the `$_SESSION` value very recently, and the `$_COOKIE` value has not been updated. If we assigned the cookie with the same value of `$_COOKIE`, the web page would never update itself. In other words, the cookie would remain at 1 forever.

The last parameter refers to how long the cookie will last. We set it for 60 * 60 * 24 * 30, which can also be read as simply 30 days. After that time, the cookie disappears and the counter resets. You can change the expire time.

The last few lines of code simply echo out the number of times the counter has been echoed. Check out what this page looks like in Figure 13.19.

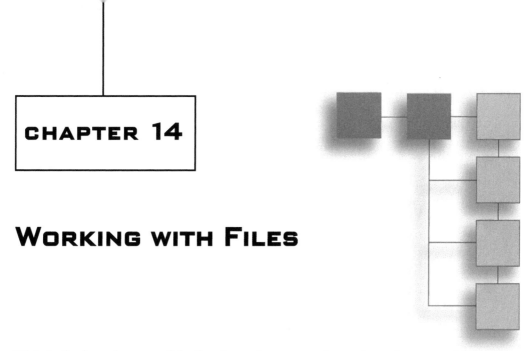

CHAPTER 14

WORKING WITH FILES

This is the last chapter of the book, and we are going to be going out with a bang. In this chapter, I'm going to teach you how to deal with files in PHP. We will now be able to accept uploads, write to files, save information, and do other cool stuff.

You might be thinking that this is exactly the same as cookies. Yeah, with cookies you can save some information about a user. However, you could only save a specific type of data; with file handling, you can save whatever information you like to the server. You can also let the user upload files directly to the server. File handling allows uploads and enables you to write to files on the user's computer.

Allowing File Uploads

You want a way for readers to communicate with you through your web site. This is commonly done through email, but sometimes the visitor may want to send something—a picture or a music file, perhaps. PHP allows you to upload a file through a form and send it to the web server. Let's take a look at how to do this.

Remember that when using forms you can choose either GET or POST. PHP file uploading works best with POST.

HTML Program

I've created the form that allows for selecting a file. This one allows you to select a file from anywhere on your computer, and then it creates a submit button that lets the visitor send the file through the browser. Check out the code that makes this happen, then look at Figure 14.1.

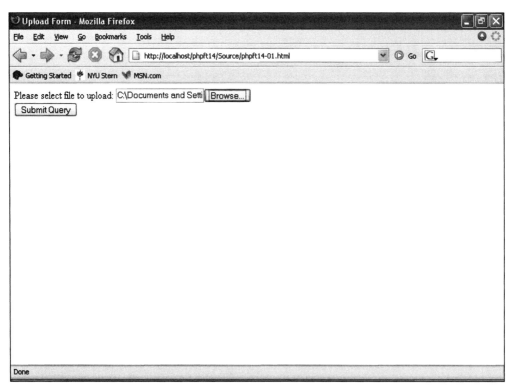

Figure 14.1
The file upload input form.

```
<!DOCTYPE html PUBLIC "-//W3C//DTD XHTML 1.0 Strict//EN"
    "http://www.w3.org/TR/xhtml1/DTD/xhtml1-strict.dtd">

<html>
<head>
<title>Upload Form</title>
</head>

<body>
<form action="phpft14-01.php" method="POST" enctype="multipart/form-data">

    <input type="hidden" name="MAX_FILE_SIZE" value="30000" >
```

```
    Please select file to upload: <input name="filename" type="file" >

    <br><input type="submit">
</form>
</body>

</html>
```

enctype

Notice that the form has several familiar parts, such as method and action, but there is something special: enctype. What is this? enctype stands for *encoding type,* and it tells the PHP server that the form is going to send something other than regular text and field data. Instead, it sends a data file called *form-data.*

input

Another weird thing is the first input inside the form, with type being set to hidden. This input parameter defines the file's maximum size. Right now, it is set to 30,000 bytes. You can adjust this to any value you like by altering the value parameter. Just make sure that the name of this input field is MAX_FILE_SIZE.

It is important you use MAX_FILE_SIZE. It prevents any uploaded file from being over the specified size. Someone can try to upload gigantic files that can use up your file space or server bandwidth. If someone has malicious intent, he can use file-uploading forms in what is called a *denial-of-service (DoS) attack.*

Browse

Lastly, because it is a file-upload form, the last field has a type of file, which creates a Browse button that lets the user select a file to upload. A box pops up like the one in Figure 14.2 when you press the Browse button.

Writing the HTML page that sends the file to the server is the easy part. Let's make the PHP program to write it permanently to the server!

PHP Program

Take a look at the PHP you need to deal with file uploads.

Arrays

When submitting a file through a form, the server creates an array that holds the uploaded files. Remember when we used sessions and had the $_SESSION array?

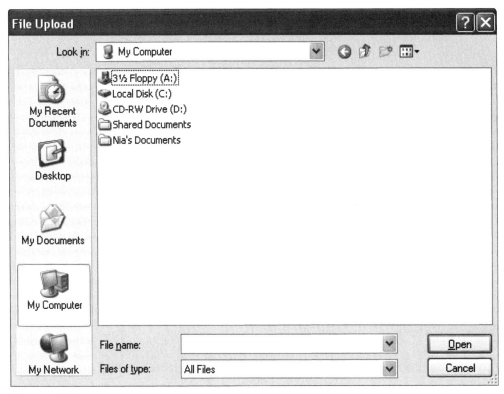

Figure 14.2
The file-upload dialog box on a file-upload field.

It's a lot like that. The $_FILES array stores five pieces of information about the uploaded data. These data are stored in multidimensional arrays:

- The first dimension is the name of the input field from the form on the previous page. (In the preceding example the field name was filename.)

- The second dimension is the name of the information field.

Table 14.1 lists the five options. You won't use all of these, but keep in mind that you have the option to use any of them whenever necessary.

move_uploaded_file()

When a file is uploaded to your server, it is placed in a temporary directory. This directory is a standard temporary directory, unless you change the upload_tmp_dir in the php.ini file. You generally don't need to change the

Table 14.1 The $_FILES Array

Array	Description
$_FILES['filename']['name']	Stores the name of the original file from the sender's computer.
$_FILES['filename']['type']	This is the MIME file type, defined by the browser. video/mpeg is an example. Figure 14.3 shows www.iana.org/assignments/media-types, where you can find out more.
$_FILES['filename']['size']	The uploaded file's size in bytes.
$_FILES['filename'] ['tmp_name']	When uploaded, a file is given a name on the server. This field stores the name of the temporary file. The file is quickly moved and no longer temporary after the full action is complete.
$_FILES['filename']['error']	This is the error code, if any, associated with the uploaded file.

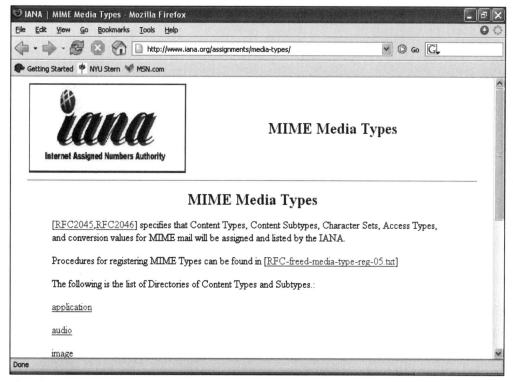

Figure 14.3
The MIME-type web site.

temporary directory. We need to move the file from the temporary directory to a directory of our choice. To do this, we can use a PHP function called `move_uploaded_file()`. The declaration for this function follows:

```
move_uploaded_file($filename, $destination)
```

Both *$filename* and *$destination* are strings that hold the path and name of the file.

To use this function, we use the `$FILES['filename']['tmp_name']` data in the array as the beginning $filename and the name of the original file as the final destination. Let's make this happen. First of all, we need to define the folder on the server where the file will be located. We can then tag on the filename to get the file's full $destination. Let's look at how this might be done:

```
$destinationdirectory = 'C:\PHP\uploads\\'; //Can be any directory on the
   server
$destination = $updirectory . basename($_FILES['file']['name']);
```

This makes sense, right? We just created a string, $upfile, as the final $destination. You might have noticed this new function, $basename(). This function removes any directory structure from a filename and returns the actual filename. So, if you were to input `basename(''C:\windows\desktop\index.html'')`, the function would return `index.html` as a string.

Note

This program only works if you have your directory set to read/write by anyone. If you are using a UNIX server, you must `chmod` the final directory to 777. Otherwise, make sure anyone has read/write privileges on the directory.

Now that we have this string created, we can use the `move_uploaded_file()` function! Two cool things to note:

- If you use this function and it returns an error (for whatever reason), the function returns a Boolean `false`; if it is successful, it returns `true`.

- You'll notice the new function `print_r()`, which prints out all the information about an array in one command.

Put it all together to make our final document:

```
<?

$updirectory = "c:\php\uploads\\"; //Can be any directory on the server
$upfile = $updirectory . basename($_FILES['file']['name']);
echo $upfile;

echo "<pre>";
if (move_uploaded_file($_FILES['file']['tmp_name'],$upfile))
{
    echo "Congrats! File was uploaded!";
}

else
{
    echo "File was not uploaded. There was an error.";

}

echo "Let's see some info about the file!";
print_r($_FILES);
echo "</pre>";

?>
```

Pretty cool huh? Figure 14.4 shows the results if you uploaded a file called test.txt.

Not too shabby. The program tries to move the file and then tells the user if the uploading was successful. Notice the code at the end of the document:

```
echo "Let's see some info about the file!";
print_r($_FILES);
echo "</pre>";
```

This function, print_r(), writes out the contents of an array in human read-able terms. As you can see in Figure 14.4, this function prints the array as follows:

```
[file] => Array
    (
        [name] => test.txt
        [type] => text/plain
```

```
            [tmp_name] => C:\PHP\uploadtemp\phpC9.tmp
            [error] => 0
            [size] => 4
    )
```

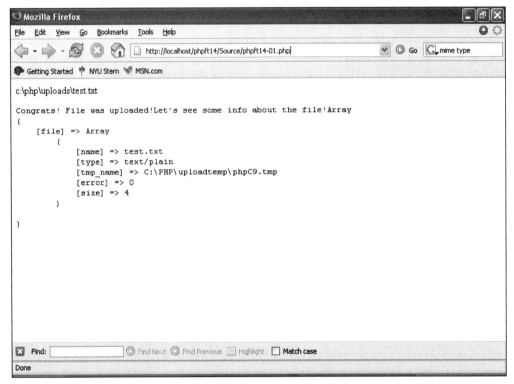

Figure 14.4
Results of uploading through `phpft14-01.php`.

This explains everything there is to know about the file. Notice the use of the `<pre></pre>` tag. This tag makes the new lines in the document's HTML code appear as new lines on the web browser screen, rather than simply disappearing. Without it, the program would look like Figure 14.5. Looks a lot harder to read, huh?

Loading Files

Opening and loading files are very common programming operations, and fortunately they are not difficult.

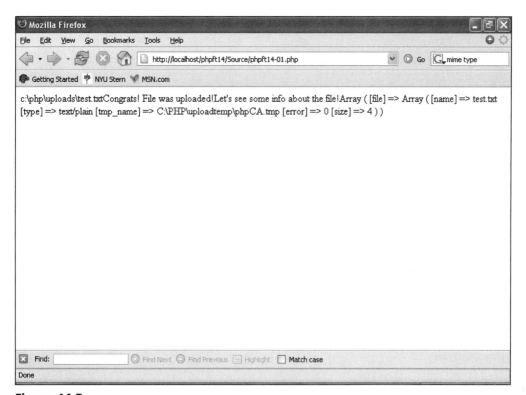

Figure 14.5
Removing the <pre> tag.

Opening a File

Opening a file requires the use of the fopen() function, which gives you access to any file and its contents. Let's look at its declaration:

```
fopen($filename, $mode)
```

Both parameters are strings. Obviously $filename is intuitive; however, $mode is a little bit more complex. Let's take a look and let me explain what that parameter means.

When you open a file, you can open it for several purposes—the most common are reading and writing. You can also open a file for *appending*, which means that you can add information only to the end of a file. Table 14.2 shows what the PHP manual has to say about all the possible modes.

There aren't too many modes. Yeah, there are two more modes, x and x+, which look weird, but because they aren't used much, I won't spend any time on them in this chapter.

Table 14.2 fopen() Modes

Mode	Description
r	This opens the file for reading only. The file pointer is put at the beginning of the file.
r+	This opens the file for reading and writing. The file pointer is put at the beginning of the file.
w	This opens the file for writing only. The file pointer is put at the beginning of the file. If the file does not exist, this attempts to create it.
w+	This opens the file for reading and writing. The file pointer is put at the beginning of the file. If the file does not exist, this attempts to create it.
a	This opens the file for writing only. The file pointer is put at the end of the file. If the file does not exist, this attempts to create it.
a+	This opens the file for reading and writing. The file pointer is put at the end of the file. If the file does not exist, this attempts to create it.

Only use the most limited of modes depending on your situation. If you need to use a file because you need to read data from it, use the r mode. If you need to create and write a file, use w. Even though you can use w+ to read or write to the file, it is safer to use the mode that allows only what you need. Otherwise, you can accidentally overwrite a file.

The fopen() function returns a handle to the file. A *handle* is essentially the same as a variable, and it stores all the data inside the file. So, if you wanted to open a file for reading, you could do it like this:

```
$file = fopen('file.txt', 'r');
```

All later operations are done upon the $file handle variable.

Closing a File

When you are done with a file inside your PHP program, close it. If you leave it open, the script can take up more space and slow down the system. Use the fclose() function to close the file. The declaration for this function is as follows:

```
fclose($handle);
```

Simply pass the variable that you retrieved from fopen() to fclose() to close the file, and the file disappears! Loading and closing a file could be done as follows:

```
<?
$handle = fopen('file.txt','w');
```

```
//Do file operations, all writing because of mode

fclose($handle);
?>
```

Writing to Files

Writing to files is almost as simple as loading and closing files. All you need is another function: fwrite(). This naming scheme is getting pretty easy to figure out, huh? Take a look at the fwrite() declaration:

```
fwrite($handle, $string)
```

With this function, you can write whatever string you want to a file. Note that we are writing an ASCII file, which means that anything you write to the file is a string, because it will be interpreted as a string when data is later read from the document. fwrite() only works if the $handle was opened for write or append access, as discussed earlier in this chapter.

So let's create a web page that lets the user append text to the bottom of a file and close it. Let's start off with the HTML form we need to create:

```
<!DOCTYPE html PUBLIC "-//W3C//DTD XHTML 1.0 Strict//EN"
    "http://www.w3.org/TR/xhtml1/DTD/xhtml1-strict.dtd">

<html>
<head>
<title>Append Form</title>
</head>

<body>
<form action="phpft14-02.php" method="POST" >

The text that you enter will be appended to the file phpft14-02.txt.

    <p>Enter text to append: <textarea name="appendedtext"></textarea>

    <br><input type="submit">
</form>
</body>

</html>
```

Check out how this looks in Figure 14.6.

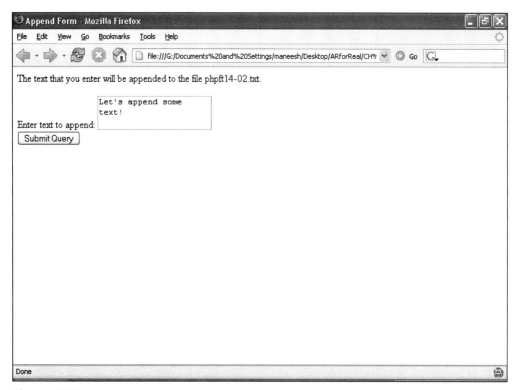

Figure 14.6
The `phpft14-02.html` appending form.

Now for the appending script, which, if working correctly, looks like Figure 14.7:

```
<?

$text = $_POST['appendedtext'];
$filename="phpft14-02.txt";

$handle = fopen($filename, 'a');

//if there is a problem with opening file, echo out error
if (!$handle)
    {
    exit("Could not open file!");
    }
```

```
//If there is an error with writing, echo out an error
if (!fwrite($handle,stripslashes($text)))
    {
    exit("Could not write data!");
    }

echo "Congratulations! Data appended!";

fclose($handle);


?>
```

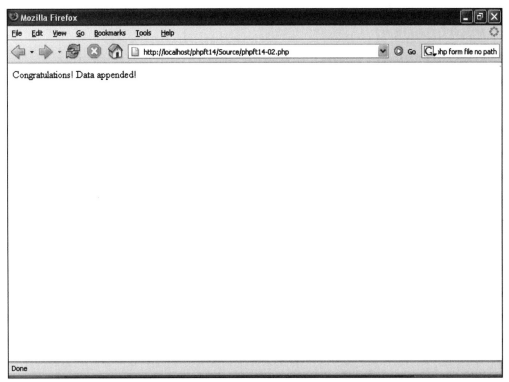

Figure 14.7
The phpft14-02.php appending script.

Check out what happens to the text file. In this example, my original document was C:\test.txt. Originally, before running the script, the file looked like the one in Figure 14.8. But after running the script, look at test.txt now, in Figure 14.9!

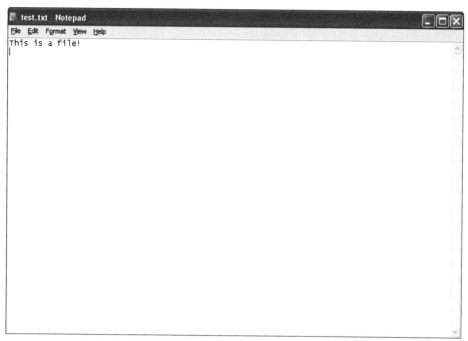

Figure 14.8
The original test.txt file.

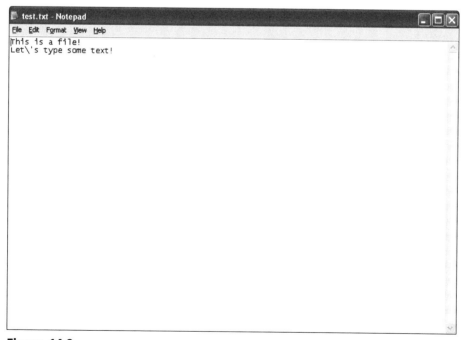

Figure 14.9
The new and appended test.txt file.

Cool, huh? But what's up with that slash in Let\'s? Characters that require escape sequences, such as the apostrophe, have a backslash before the character. Fortunately, there is an easy way to fix this. PHP includes a cool function: stripslashes().

```
stripslashes($string)
```

This function removes all the backslashes from a string and returns the new string. If we wanted to add this to our document, we would only need to change one line. We would change our fwrite() line from this

```
if (!fwrite($handle,$text))
```

to this

```
if (!fwrite($handle,stripslashes($text)))
```

After doing so, you can see what the new test.txt file would look like in Figure 14.10. Small changes make big differences, huh?

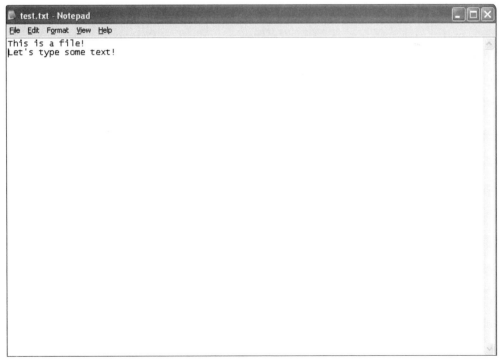

Figure 14.10
Using stripslashes().

Reading in Files

Reading in files is almost the same as writing to files—just the opposite. When we were writing to files earlier, we passed a string as a parameter that contained the data in the file. When we read in files, the reading function returns a string that we can manipulate for our purposes.

fread()

So what is the reading function, then? If you've been paying attention, you can probably guess the name: fread(). Take a look at the function declaration:

```
fread($handle, $lengthInBytes)
```

Both of these parameters are required. The first parameter is the handle to the file we retrieved by using fopen(). The second parameter is the number of bytes you wish to retrieve. fread() only works for pages that have been opened for reading access.

This sounds all well and good if you know the amount of data you need to retrieve, but what if you don't? What if you want to retrieve the entire file? Fortunately, PHP gives you a way to do this. PHP's filesize() function returns a file's size in bytes. Look at the declaration:

```
filesize($filename)
```

Pretty cool, huh? If you want to read in an entire file, you can do it as follows:

```
$contents = fread($handle, filesize($filename));
```

There are a couple other cool functions you should know about. One is fgets(), which reads the file until the next carriage return, returning the current line. You can call this inside a loop and display or act upon the entire contents of a file.

file()

Another cool function is file(), which takes the entire file into an array without requiring an fopen() command! All you have to do is pass file() the filename, as follows:

```
$entireFile = file("yourfile.txt");
```

This creates an array of each line of the file. As an alternative, you can use a foreach loop and act upon each line of the file.

After running this line of code, the $contents variable contains the entire contents of the $handle file. The contents are in string format. You can do all of your operations upon the strings, as I explain in Chapter 8.

So let's use all of this in a script. You know by now how to make the HTML document, but feel free to take a look at phpft14-03.html to see how the HTML looks. The page we made looks like the one in Figure 14.11.

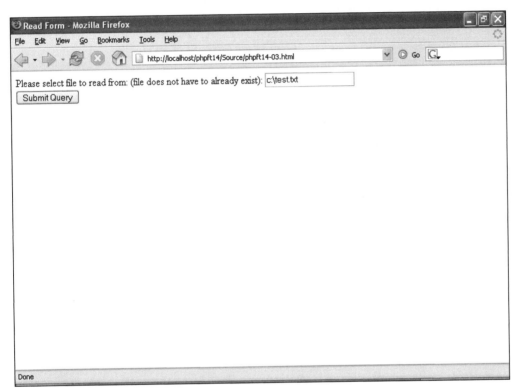

Figure 14.11
The phpft14-03.html reading form.

Now look at the PHP code that makes the reading happen:

```
<?

$filename = "c:\\test.txt";//$_POST['file'];

$handle = fopen($filename, 'r');
//if there is a problem with opening file, echo out error
if (!$handle)
```

```
        {
        exit("Could not open file!");
        }

$contents = fread($handle,filesize($filename));

//If there is an error with writing, echo out an error
if (!$contents)
        {
        exit("Could not read data!");
        }

echo "The contents of your file $filename follow.<p>";
echo $contents;

fclose($handle);

?>
```

The main thing is the fread() line:

```
$contents = fread($handle,filesize($filename));
```

Here, we pass the $handle and the filesize of the file to the fread() function. We put the result of this operation into the $contents variable. After this we check to see if $contents is valid by running the following if test:

```
if (!$contents)
        {
        exit("Could not read data!");
        }
```

$contents is invalid if it is blank, so we can check to see if it is valid by doing the above test. If the file is blank, the program exits. Cool, huh? You can do whatever you like with the file, maybe remove all of the new lines, or search for specific substrings, or whatever you feel like!

Renaming, Copying, and Deleting Files

There are only a few more functions that I want to go over before finishing off this chapter. These three functions are commonly used in file situations, both on a computer and on a web site. They are simple to use, and all return a Boolean value. If the function is successful, the function returns true; if it is false, the function returns false.

copy

The first function copies:

```
copy($source_filename, $destination_filename)
```

When using the copy function, the program knows already that the source file needs to be opened for reading and the destination file needs to be open for writing. Because of this, the function does not require that you pass in a handle of a file, but just the filename. The function actually sends the copy and rename commands to the operating system, delegating the work from the PHP program—saves you some work.

rename

The second function renames:

```
rename($old_filename, $new_filename);
```

One cool thing to know about rename is that you can use it to move a file across directories, as well. By renaming the file to have a different path, you can move the file. For example, if the old filename is C:\test.txt and the new filename is D:\text\test.txt, you move the file from the C:\ directory to D:\text. Pretty nifty, huh?

unlink

The last function deletes files. I bet you think you know what the function name is.

```
unlink($filename)
```

Weird, huh? PHP sometimes gives functions annoying names, so even though most people would expect this function to be delete(), it is instead entitled unlink().

These functions are all simple to use, and all return a Boolean value. If the function is successful, the function returns true, and if it is false, the function returns false.

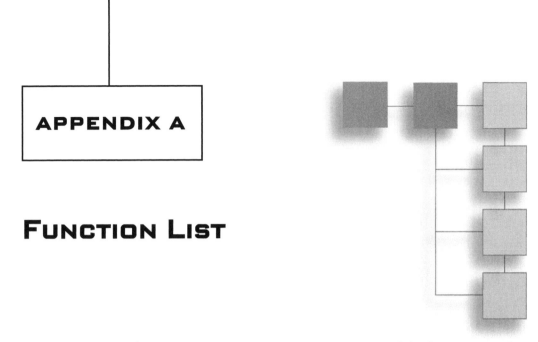

APPENDIX A

FUNCTION LIST

This appendix lists all of the descriptions and declarations of the functions in this book. The declaration is described as follows:

returnType FunctionName(varType variable1, varType variable2, . . .)

All of the functions follow this pattern. If the function returns nothing, the return type is `void`. If the parameter is optional, brackets are placed around the parameter.

Table A.1 Functions

Name	Description	Code
basename()	Returns the filename component of a filename string.	string basename(string $fullString)
copy()	Copies the contents of one file to another.	bool copy(string $source_filename, string $destination_filename)
define()	Takes in a constant name and a constant value and defines the constant in the program.	void define(string $constantName, int constantValue);

continued

Table A.1 continued

Name	Description	Code
echo	Although this is not a function (it is a language construct), it acts as one. Outputs the specified text or variable to the page.	`void echo (string $1, . . . .)`
exit	Although this is not a function (it is a language construct), it acts as one. Causes the PHP page to immediately halt script execution. No following PHP commands are executed on the page.	`void exit (string/int $status);`
fclose()	Closes a file.	`void fclose(resource $handle);`
filesize()	Returns the size of a file in bytes.	`int filesize(string $filename);`
fopen()	Opens a file and returns a handle to it.	`resource fopen(string $filename, string $mode)`
fread()	Returns a string that contains all the contents inside the chosen file.	`string fread(resource $handle, int $sizeInBytes);`
fwrite()	Writes a string to an already opened file.	`bool fwrite(resource $handle, string $text);`
gettype()	Returns the type of the inputted variable.	`string gettype(anytype $variable);`
header()	Allows you to modify some section of the document header. Using the `Location:` attribute changes the web page's URL.	`void header(string $newLocation);`
isset()	Confirms whether a variable has been created. Returns `true` if it already exists and `false` if not.	`bool isset(anytype $variable);`
mail()	Lets your web server send an email message.	`bool mail(string $to, string $subject, string $message, [string $additionalheaders], [string $additionalparameters])`
move_uploaded_file()	Moves a file from its temporary location to its final destination on your server.	`bool move_uploaded_file (string $source, string $destination);`
nl2br()	Takes in a string as a parameter and converts the new lines into ` ` tags. Allows proper display of strings in the web browser.	`string nl2br(string $text);`
rename()	Renames a file.	`bool rename(string $old_filename, string $new_filename);`

Table A.1 concluded

Name	Description	Code
session_ name()	Allows you to assign a name to your session. Includes a string parameter to change the name. If you leave the parameter blank, the current session's name is returned.	`string session_name ([string $name]);`
session_ start()	Initiates or continues using a session. This function must be placed before any other echoed HTML or text.	`void session_start(void);`
setcookie()	Sets a cookie on the web server, which lets you store user data.	`bool setcookie(string, $name, [string $value, int $expire, string $path, string $domain, bool $secure])`
stripslashes()	Returns a string with all backslashes removed.	`string stripslashes(string $orginalString);`
strval()	Takes in a non-string as a parameter and returns the input as a string value.	`string strval(int $nonstring);`
time()	Returns the number of seconds since the epoch (returns the current time).	`int time(void);`
unlink()	Deletes a file.	`bool unlink(string $filename)`
unset()	Deletes an element of an array or an entire array, depending on what variable you pass.	`void unset(anytype $elementOrArray);`

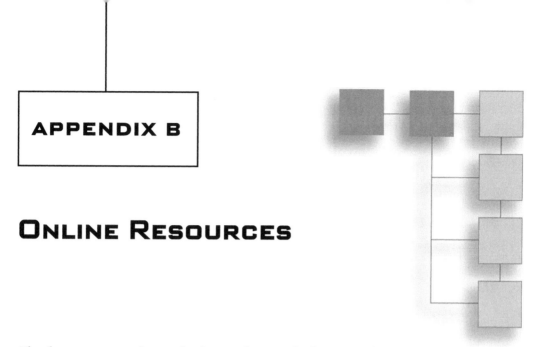

APPENDIX B

ONLINE RESOURCES

Check out some other web sites to learn a little more about PHP once you are done with this book. Here are some recommendations:

- www.php.net—This is the official PHP web site. You can read the documentation or see a full and complete function list. The tutorial is excellent.

- php.resourceindex.com—This is a great resource for working PHP scripts and tutorials. You can find a lot of cool tips and hacks.

- www.courseptr.com—This site offers books that can take your PHP and SQL/MySQL studies to a higher level.

- www.maneeshsethi.com—This is my web site and I've included some information for this book. Go to www.maneeshsethi.com/forum to interact with other readers.

APPENDIX C

WHAT'S ON THE CD

On this book's CD, you find all of the source code for all of the chapters. In addition, it offers the Nvu HTML editor and a few cool PHP editors. The CD is laid out like this:

```
Source/
     Chapter 01/
     Chapter 02/
     . . .
     Chapter 14
Programs/
Extra Programs/
```

Just navigate to the directory of your choice to install the software. The Programs directory contains Apache and PHP for installation on your machine. The Extra Programs directory holds the editors.

INDEX

Symbols

{ } (curly braces), **88, 90**
\r (carriage return), **131**
$ (dollar sign), **61**
. (dot operator), **75, 83, 92–93**
= (equal) operator, **90**
/ (forward slash), **27**
> (greater than), **61, 90**
>= (greater than or equal to) operator, **90**
\t (horizontal tab), **131**
< (less than), **61, 90**
<= (less than or equal to) operator, **90**
\n (line feed), **131**
; (semicolon), **12, 64–65**
' (single quotation marks), **75**
_ (underscore), **66, 100**

A

A Guide to MySQL (Pratt), **211**
A Guide to SQL (Last and Pratt), **211**
a+ mode, fopen() function, **232**
a mode, fopen() function, **232**
action attribute
   advanced forms, 171–172
   <form> tag, 44, 52
<alt> tag, **37**
Apache services monitor, PHP installation, **6**
apostrophes, **125**
appending files, **231**
arithmetic operators, **83–85**
array data type, **60**
arrays
   array() function, 152
   $arrayname value, 162
   creation, 151–152

   defined, 71–72
   element creation, 153
   for loop and, 157–158
   keys in, 151, 154–157
   numeric indices for, 157
   old values, removing, 158–160
   reference items, 152–153
   return values, 152
ASCII files, **25**
assignment operator, **91**

B

<b> tag, **33**
basename() function, **243**
binary operators, **81**
Binary option, PHP installation, **4**
blank sentences in forms, **58**
<body> tag, **28**
bolded text, **33**
boolean data type, **60**

 tag, **37, 124**
branching structures, control
   structures, **103–104**
break statements, **113, 120**

C

C++, comment use, **101**
C method, comment use, **101**
capitalization
   constant naming rules, 78
   style considerations, 99–100
   variable naming rules, 66
carriage return (\r), **131**
Cascading Style Sheets (CSS), **33**

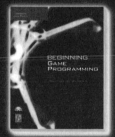

Get Ready to Rock Your Gadget!

Got a new gadget? Use it like a pro right away with these hot new guides!

The Gadget Geek's Guide is a no frills, get-down-to-business series for users who want to make the most of their gadget's features **now**! Each book includes quick tips designed to help you conquer each feature in no time. You'll also get insider advice on techniques used by advanced "techno junkies" who have come up with cool new ways to use the technology. You'll be amazed by what your gadget can do!

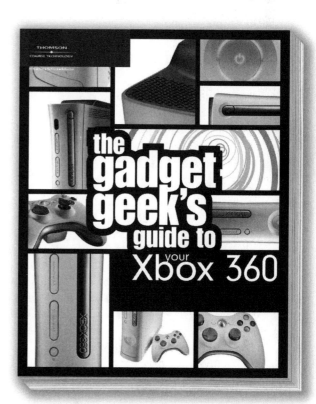

The Gadget Geek's Guide to Your Xbox 360

ISBN: 1-59863-173-X ■ $19.99

Also Available

The Gadget Geek's Guide to Portable Media Devices

ISBN: 1-59863-169-1 ■ $19.99

The Gadget Geek's Guide to Your Sony PlayStation Portable

ISBN: 1-59863-236-1 ■ $21.99

The Gadget Geek's Guide to Your BlackBerry and Trēo

ISBN: 1-59863-171-3 ■ $19.99

Call **1 888 270 0300** to order ■ Order online at **www.courseptr.com**

License Agreement/Notice of Limited Warranty

By opening the sealed disc container in this book, you agree to the following terms and conditions. If, upon reading the following license agreement and notice of limited warranty, you cannot agree to the terms and conditions set forth, return the unused book with unopened disc to the place where you purchased it for a refund.

License

The enclosed software is copyrighted by the copyright holder(s) indicated on the software disc. You are licensed to copy the software onto a single computer for use by a single user and to a backup disc. You may not reproduce, make copies, or distribute copies or rent or lease the software in whole or in part, except with written permission of the copyright holder(s). You may transfer the enclosed disc only together with this license, and only if you destroy all other copies of the software and the transferee agrees to the terms of the license. You may not decompile, reverse assemble, or reverse engineer the software.

Notice of Limited Warranty

The enclosed disc is warranted by Thomson Course Technology PTR to be free of physical defects in materials and workmanship for a period of sixty (60) days from end user's purchase of the book/disc combination. During the sixty-day term of the limited warranty, Thomson Course Technology PTR will provide a replacement disc upon the return of a defective disc.

Limited Liability

THE SOLE REMEDY FOR BREACH OF THIS LIMITED WARRANTY SHALL CONSIST ENTIRELY OF REPLACEMENT OF THE DEFECTIVE DISC. IN NO EVENT SHALL THOMSON COURSE TECHNOLOGY PTR OR THE AUTHOR BE LIABLE FOR ANY OTHER DAMAGES, INCLUDING LOSS OR CORRUPTION OF DATA, CHANGES IN THE FUNCTIONAL CHARACTERISTICS OF THE HARDWARE OR OPERATING SYSTEM, DELETERIOUS INTERACTION WITH OTHER SOFTWARE, OR ANY OTHER SPECIAL, INCIDENTAL, OR CONSEQUENTIAL DAMAGES THAT MAY ARISE, EVEN IF THOMSON COURSE TECHNOLOGY PTR AND/OR THE AUTHOR HAS PREVIOUSLY BEEN NOTIFIED THAT THE POSSIBILITY OF SUCH DAMAGES EXISTS.

Disclaimer of Warranties

THOMSON COURSE TECHNOLOGY PTR AND THE AUTHOR SPECIFICALLY DISCLAIM ANY AND ALL OTHER WARRANTIES, EITHER EXPRESS OR IMPLIED, INCLUDING WARRANTIES OF MERCHANTABILITY, SUITABILITY TO A PARTICULAR TASK OR PURPOSE, OR FREEDOM FROM ERRORS. SOME STATES DO NOT ALLOW FOR EXCLUSION OF IMPLIED WARRANTIES OR LIMITATION OF INCIDENTAL OR CONSEQUENTIAL DAMAGES, SO THESE LIMITATIONS MIGHT NOT APPLY TO YOU.

Other

This Agreement is governed by the laws of the State of Massachusetts without regard to choice of law principles. The United Convention of Contracts for the International Sale of Goods is specifically disclaimed. This Agreement constitutes the entire agreement between you and Thomson Course Technology PTR regarding use of the software.